The Great Pantyhose Crafts Book

Ed & Stevie Baldwin

Created by The Family Workshop, Inc.

Art Director: D. Curtis Hale
Photography: Ed Baldwin
Project Designs: April Bail and Stevie Baldwin
Production: Chris Berg, Alan Harcrow, Jacqueline Nelson, Roberta Taff
Editing: Sue Puckitt

For Western Publishing Company, Inc.

Jonathan P. Latimer, Editorial Director, Adult Books

Notice: The information in this book is true and complete to the best of our knowledge. All recommendations are made without guarantees on the part of the authors or Western Publishing Co., Inc. The authors and Western Publishing Co., Inc. disclaim all liability in connection with the use of this information.

Published by: Western Publishing Company, Inc.
850 Third Avenue
New York, New York 10022

ISBN: 0-307-46616-7 (SOFT), 0-307-46615-9 (HARD)
Library of Congress Catalog Card Number: 82-81366
© 1982 The Family Workshop, Inc. Printed in U.S.A.

Hosiery products for all projects in this book were provided by:
L'eggs Products, Inc.
P. O. Box 2495
Winston-Salem, N.C. 27102
The nurse's white hose are available by mail order only.
The heavy "winter" hose are not available all year.

Additional craft patterns are available from The Family Workshop, Inc. For a catalog, send $1.50 to: The Family Workshop, Department 10017, P.O. Box 52000, Tulsa, Oklahoma 74152

This book is dedicated in loving memory to
Dorothy Lillian Baldwin

Foreword

I must confess that I have very little grasp of the current world situation. I am unable to deal effectively with our world balance of payments, international terrorism, or even which countries should be admitted to the United Nations. Bigger minds than mine are contemplating life on other planets. The problems that I tackle, however, loom larger than mere world or interplanetary questions. In particular, they concern the problem of what to do with a pair of pantyhose which have served me well, but have developed a giant-sized run.

In this book, you will find 40 different ways to recycle hose and give them a second life as useful and decorative projects for your home, for gifts, for bazaars, or just for fun.

I still do not expect you to run headlong into evergreen bushes wearing your new hose in order to make these projects. However, Ed and I both will feel a sense of accomplishment if you are not quite as depressed when you get that next run.

Stevie Baldwin

Table of Contents

TIPS & TECHNIQUES   4

RIBBONS & BOWS
gifts & bazaar items for everyone
Baby Doll   9
Riding Horse   13
Picture Frame   16
Ribbon Comb   20
"I Love You" Pillow   22
Grandmother's Keepsake   25
Little Black Evening Bag   28
Ski Vest and Hat   30

KID STUFF
for that special child
Child's Keepsake Picture   35
Toddler Toys   37
Birth Record   40
Crib Comforter   43
Ned & Nell   45
Circus Crib Mobile   55
Animal Slippers   62
Ballerina Marionette   64

THE PERFECT TOUCH
for your home decor
The Gork   73
Coiled Rug   80
"Granny" & "Shady Lady"   82
Pantyhose Cactus   88
Sculptured Head   91
Snow Dove   94
Footstool   97
Magical Unicorn   99

CELEBRATIONS
sparkling additions to special occasions
Halloween Ghost & Pumpkin   105
Bridal Shower Centerpiece   108
Christi Christmas Witch   111
Santa & Mrs. Claus   113
Easter Table Centerpiece   119
Christmas Ornaments   122
Thanksgiving Turkey   128
Christmas Treetop Angel   132
Christmas Wreath   136

KITCHEN SPICE
added flavorings where you cook
Kitchen Witch   141
Katie T. Cozy & Tea Container   145
Fantasy Flowers   148
Taste Makes Waist   150
Hot Pad, Drink Coaster, & Napkin Ring   153
Casserole Carrier   156
Kitchen Pictures   158

Tips & Techniques

hints to help you on your way

Enlarging a pattern

To enlarge a design, draw 1-inch squares on a large piece of paper, in the same arrangement as the original grid. Copy the original design to the larger grid, working square by square **(Figure A).** Transfer the enlarged design to fabric or other surface using carbon paper and a pencil.

Fabric painting

Acrylic paint straight from the tube is usually a good thickness for fabric painting. If the paint begins to dry while you are working with it, add a drop of water and stir thoroughly. A paint that is too watery will bleed into the fabric; paint that is too thick will not penetrate the fibers.

A single small brush is enough to begin fabric painting. You may want to add larger brushes later. Good brushes are expensive, but are well worth the money.

Embroidery

Cotton embroidery thread contains 6 strands which can be easily separated. The fewer strands you use, the smaller needle you need, the more stitches you will take, and the finer the finished work.

To avoid knotting the thread at the beginning of embroidery, work a running stitch on the surface, positioning it so that subsequent stitches will cover it. Finish a length of thread by running the end under the last few stitches. Always use an embroidery hoop to hold your fabric while you work. We also suggest that you preshrink your fabric.

1 or 2 strands of embroidery thread can be threaded easily if you moisten them first. When using more than 2 strands (or large thread), fold 1 over the eye of the needle. Pinch the fold tightly between the thumb and forefinger and pull the needle out. Still holding the tightly-pinched fold, thread the eye of the needle down over it. When the fold is threaded, you can pull the rest of the yarn through easily.

Illustrations for each of the embroidery stitches are given in **Figure B.** With a little practice, even a beginner can produce stitches that are smooth and uniform.

Figure A

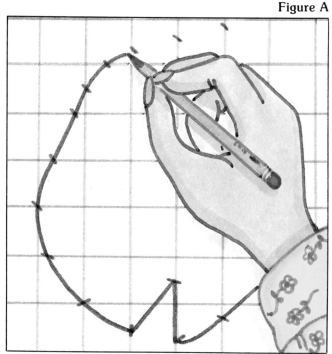

4

Figure B

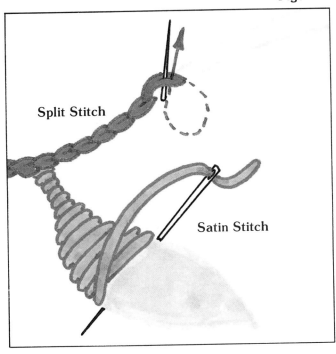

Split Stitch

Satin Stitch

Figure C

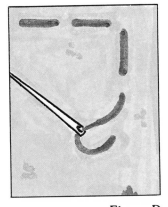

Figure D

Figure E

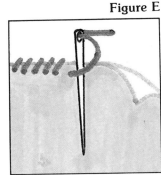

Figure F

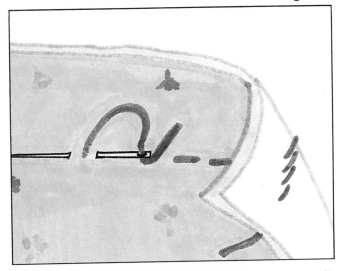

Sewing stitches

Basting Stitches are used to hold fabric in place temporarily before the final stitching is done by hand or machine, and are removed after the project is completed.

To baste, take a stitch through the fabric layers, skip a space and take another stitch **(Figure C)**. Basting stitches are usually fairly long (about ½ inch in length). For easy removal, use a thread color that will be easy to see.

Topstitching is a final stitch on the top of the fabric where it will show on the finished project **(Figure D)**. The stitching line should be very straight, and a uniform distance from the edge of the fabric.

Whipstitching joins 2 fabric pieces together, catching an equal amount of fabric on each edge **(Figure E)**. Insert the needle underneath the bottom edge. Bring the needle through the bottom fabric and diagonally forward into the top edge. Insert the needle down through the top edge, straight across through the bottom edge, and then up through the bottom edge. Each stitch is worked straight across perpendicularly to the fabric edges, resulting in a diagonal stitch pattern on the visible side of the fabric.

Backstitching is the strongest stitch you can do by hand. Insert the needle ¼ inch behind where the thread comes out, and exit ¼ inch in front **(Figure F)**. The back of your work will have long overlapping stitches. Keep the stitches equal in length.

The main thing to remember when soft sculpturing pantyhose is that you do not have to settle for what you get the first time. Stuffed hose are remarkably pliable and moldable — almost like working with clay. Even after a hose has been stuffed and tied off, you can manipulate the shape to an amazing degree. If you wish to enlarge a small area, you can use the tip of your needle to pull the fiberfill out. For larger areas, you can pull the fiberfill out using your hands. By working with the stuffed hose, you can manipulate it to assume many characteristics.

It is easier to work with a shape that has not been overstuffed. You want just enough fiberfill to fill out the desired shape, but not so much that you cut down on your working ability. If a shape is very tightly stuffed, there will be no room for the fiberfill to give when you wish to manipulate a specific shape.

When you soft-sculpture faces, use a long sharp needle and heavy-duty thread. We used a heavy thread which is usually sold for drapery making. It will take the strain of sculpture work without breaking, and is not apt to hurt your hands.

If you are just beginning, we suggest that you make a "practice" head before completing the project. This will give you more confidence in working with soft sculpture. If you put a runner in the face, or you don't like the results the first time, simply manipulate the stuffing inside the head, turn it around, and use the back of the head as the front. The first face will be covered by the hair anyway.

If you do see a runner about to develop, you can touch it with a small amount of clear nail polish, let the polish dry, and continue working.

Glueing

Ordinary white glue can be used to make all of the projects in this book. However, hot-melt adhesive is a real timesaver. This glue comes in solid sticks which are inserted in a special glue gun. The gun heats the glue sticks, and dispenses melted glue when you pull the trigger. The hot glue can be used to adhere fabric to hose, or hose to hose. It is a very quick process, and will eliminate the clamping time required for white glue. It can also be used in many applications as a substitute for hand stitching.

The glue is extremely hot when it is ejected from the gun, and will blister your fingers if you touch it before it cools. For that reason, use extreme care when working with a glue gun. Surprisingly enough, the extremely hot glue will not melt the hose.

Choosing pantyhose for projects

The specific type of pantyhose used for each project is listed in the materials specified for that project. When "regular" pantyhose is specified, any flesh-colored hose (from light to dark) may be used. The instructions assume that the hose have a reinforced toe, heel, and panty. If you use a "sandal foot" or "sheer to waist" hose, simply follow the instructions for cutting the hose as if the reinforced portions were there. When queen-size hose are specified, it is because of the size of the project and the resulting strain that is put on the hose. Regular (non-support) hose can be used if you reduce the size of the finished project.

Sewing techniques

Gathers are used wherever soft fullness is desired in a finished project, and may be done by hand or with a machine. Use a large stitch and sew 1 row of stitching close to the cut edge on the right side of the fabric, leaving the ends of the thread long. Stitch a second row close to the first.

Working on the wrong side of the fabric, pull the 2 long threads gently. Work the resulting gathers to the center of the fabric piece and adjust them evenly over that side. Repeat the process, working from the opposite end of the piece. Pull the threads gently to avoid breaking them.

Clipping seams is necessary on curves or corners so the finished project will lie flat when pressed. To eliminate excess seam allowance on an outward curve or corner, cut v-shaped notches in the seam allowance. Be careful not to cut through the seam stitches.

An inside curve must also be clipped, since there will not be enough fabric in the seam allowance to turn the curve. Clip as close to the stitching as possible without cutting through.

Working with pantyhose

When machine stitching pantyhose, always stretch the hose gently as you sew. The stretching will space your stitches so they will not break when the hose is stretched along the seam.

RIBBONS AND BOWS

... gifts & bazaar items for everyone

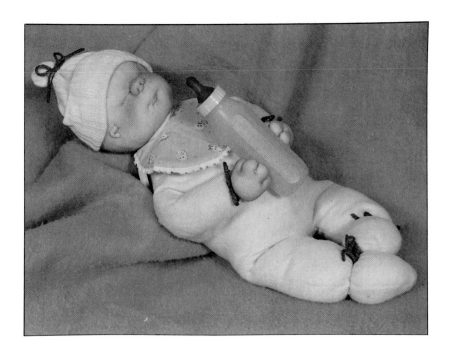

Cuddly Baby Doll

This soft and cuddly baby doll will be loved by youngsters from 1 to 91. A pattern is given for his flannel sleeper, but you can substitute a treasured baby sleeper of your own.

Materials

1 yard of cotton flannel or other soft fabric in a pastel color.
1 pair of pantyhose.
½ yard of off-white ribbed stretch fabric.
¼ yard of small print fabric.
20-inch length of white lace trim.
Scraps of blue yarn or ribbon.
18-inch length of white seam binding.
1 pound of polyester fiberfill.
Scissors, glue, ruler, a long sharp needle, and heavy-duty thread.
Powdered cheek blusher, and an eyebrow pencil or narrow felt-tip marker.
Paper and pencil to enlarge the patterns.

Making the head

1. Tie a knot at the panty line on 1 pantyhose leg. Cut the leg from the hose 1 inch above the knot **(Figure A)**. Measure 10 inches down from the knot and cut again. This 10-inch length will form the baby's head. Turn the hose inside out so the knot is on the inside.

2. Stuff the hose with generous amounts of fiberfill until the head is approximately 19 inches in circumference **(Figure B)**. Tie the hose in a knot at the "neck."

Figure A

Figure B

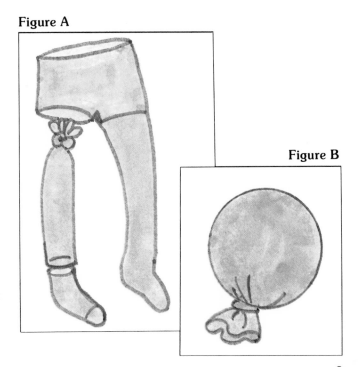

Figure C

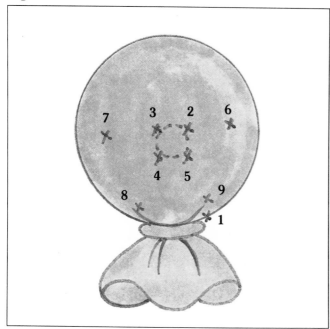

Figure D

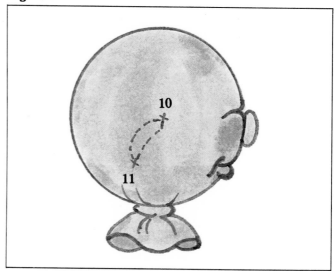

3. Follow the entry and exit points illustrated in **Figure C** to form the facial features. Use a long sharp needle and 1 long heavy-duty thread for the entire procedure.

    a. Enter at 1 and exit at 2. Sew a circle of basting stitches approximately 2 inches in diameter, exiting at 3.

    b. Use the tip of the needle to very carefully lift the fiberfill within the circle just enough to make a small bulge. Gently pull the thread until a small round nose appears.

    c. Hold the thread with 1 hand and lock the stitch under the bridge of the nose, exiting at 2.

    d. To form the nostrils, reenter at 2 and exit at 4.

    e. Reenter ¼ inch directly above 4 and exit at 3.

    f. Reenter at 3 and exit at 5.

    g. Reenter ¼ inch directly above 5 and exit at 2. Lock the stitch under the bridge of the nose.

    h. To form the eyes, enter at 2 and exit at 6.

    i. Pull the thread over the surface, enter at 2 and exit at 3.

    j. Reenter at 3 and exit at 7.

    k. Pull the thread across the surface, enter at 3 and exit at 2. Gently pull the thread until closed eyes appear, and lock the stitch.

    l. To form the mouth, enter at 2 and exit at 8.

    m. Pull the thread across the surface, enter at 9 and exit at 3. Pull the thread until the smile appears.

    n. Reenter at 3 and exit at 1. Lock the stitch and cut the thread.

    o. The bottom lip is formed by repeating the last 3 steps (l through n) just under the mouth line using a smaller stitch.

4. Brush powdered cheek blusher on cheeks and bottom lip. Dot freckles across the nose and cheeks with a narrow felt-tip marker or an eyebrow pencil.

5. Thread the needle again and follow the entry and exit points given in **Figure D** to form the ears.

    a. Pinch up a small ridge at an angle on the side of the head just below the eyeline. Enter at 1 and exit at 10. Stitch back and forth under the ridge until an ear forms.

    b. Exit at 11 and lock the stitch.

    c. Reenter at 11 and exit at 1. Lock the stitch and cut the thread.

6. Repeat step 5 on the opposite side of the head to form the other ear.

Making the body

1. Enlarge the patterns given in **Figure E** to full size. Cut 2 body pieces from the cotton flannel and 2 bib pieces from the small print fabric.

2. Sew the 2 body pieces right sides together, leaving the wrists and neck open and unstitched. Work through the neck opening to stuff the entire body. Stuff lightly but evenly until body is plump but not hard.

3. Gather the neck opening using a needle and heavy-duty thread ¼ inch from the edge. Pull the gathering threads until the opening measures approximately 2 inches in diameter and lock the stitch.

4. Center the head over the gathered neck opening. Whipstitch the head to the body, working completely around the neck several times until the head is very secure.

5. Turn under a ¼-inch hem on the raw edge of each sleeve, and whipstitch in place.

Making the hands

1. Cut a 4-inch circular piece of hose, and wrap it around a 3-inch ball of fiberfill. Tie the hose together at the bottom with thread.

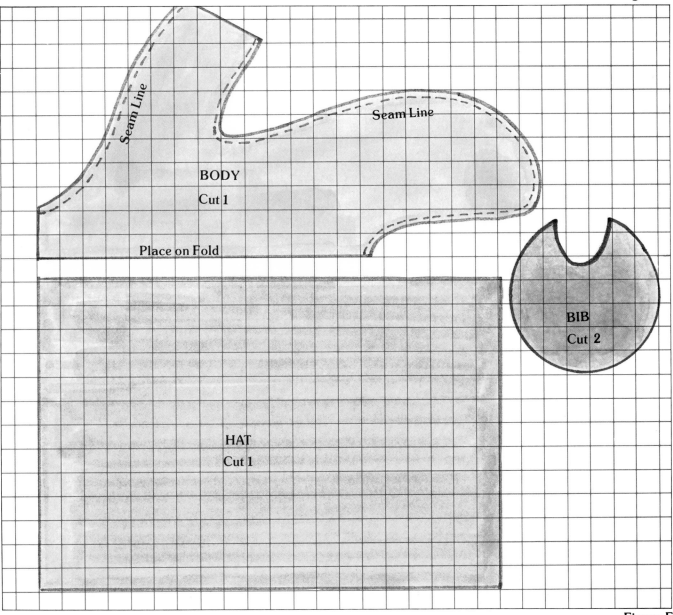

2. The fist is formed by dividing the fingers with thread. Follow the illustrations given in **Figure F** as you work.

    a. Enter the needle at 1 and exit at 2 (on what will be the back of the hand).

    b. Slightly flatten the ball of fiberfill at the top to form the finger portion of the fist. Wrap the thread over the end of the finger and insert the needle on the front side of the fist directly opposite 2. Exit at 2. Pull the stitch tightly to form the first finger.

    c. Enter at 2 and exit at 3 to begin the next finger.

    d. Again wrap the thread over the end of the finger and enter on the front side directly opposite 3. Pull the thread tightly to form the second finger.

    e. Repeat the procedure twice more at points 4 and 5 to form the last 2 fingers.

    f. Return the needle to 1 and lock the stitch.

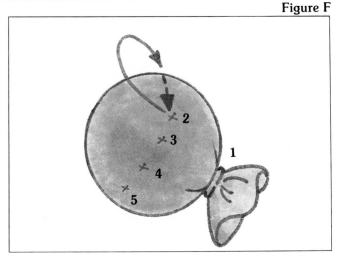

Figure J

Figure G

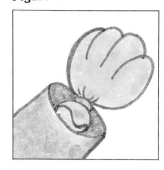

Figure H

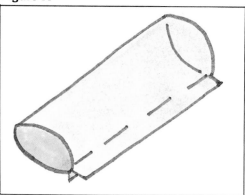

Figure I

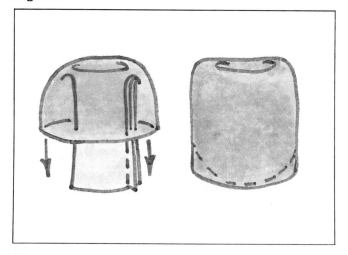

3. Place the fist over the wrist, inserting the raw edges of the hose inside the opening **(Figure G).** Whipstitch around the wrist several times to anchor the fist to the sleeve. Pull the thread to tighten, and lock the stitch.

Hat and bib

1. Cut the Hat piece from off-white ribbed stretch fabric. Fold it lengthwise with right sides together. **(Figure H).** Stitch a ¼-inch seam along the raw edge.

2. Refold the stitched tube in half back over itself so you have a double thickness with the seam on the inside and the raw edges together **(Figure I).**

3. Position the seam in the center and sew a curved seam across the raw edges as shown in Figure I. Trim the seam to ¼ inch, and turn the hat right side out.

4. Place 2 bib pieces right sides together, sandwiching the lace trim between the 2 layers **(Figure J).** Pin and stitch the curved outer edges. Turn the bib right side out and press it.

5. Encase the neck edge with seam binding, leaving a length of seam binding on both sides of the neck to tie a bow in the back.

Finishing

1. Tie bows of yarn or ribbon around wrists and 4 inches above the bottom of the foot.

2. Place the hat on the baby's head and turn the cuff back over the hat.

3. Glue the hat to the head along the front of the face.

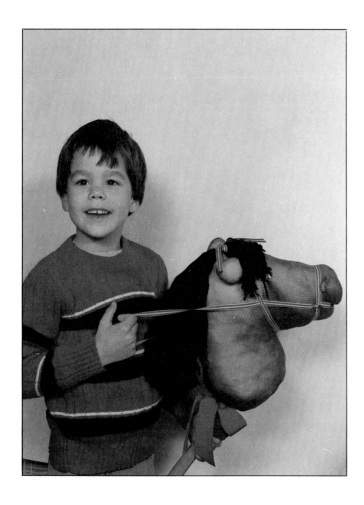

Riding Horse

For generations, children have loved stick horses. This updated version will provide hours of riding fun for any youngster.

Materials

1 pair of heavy gray-colored "winter" hose.
1 skein of black yarn.
3 yards of ½-inch-wide striped grosgrain ribbon.
1 pound of polyester fiberfill.
2 white buttons with smooth tops and a bottom shank.
10-inch length of wide black seam binding.
Black laundry marker.
Heavy-duty gray thread and a long sharp needle.
1 yard of wide red grosgrain ribbon.
1-inch-diameter wooden dowel rod, 4 feet long.
12 x 14-inch piece of heavy cardboard.
Clear acrylic spray and glue.
Small hand saw, package tape, and scissors.
Razor knife, glue, spring-type clothespins, scissors, and toothpicks.
Paper and pencil to enlarge the patterns.

Making the head

1. Use a small hand saw to cut a narrow, 6-inch-deep slot in 1 end of the dowel rod to accommodate the cardboard head, as shown in **Figure A**.

Figure A

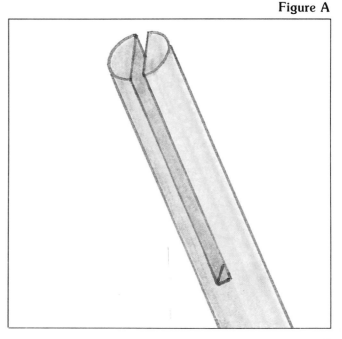

Figure B

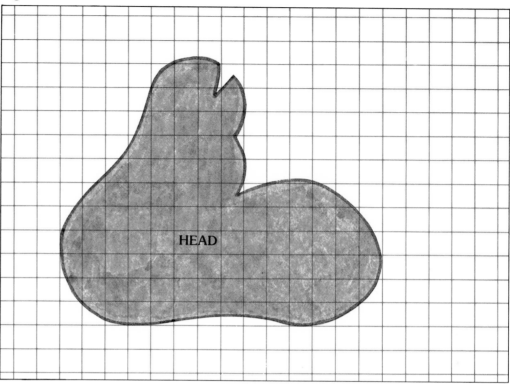

HEAD

Figure C

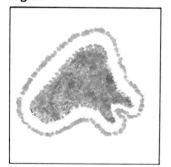

Figure D

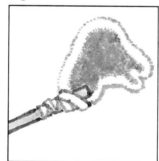

Figure E

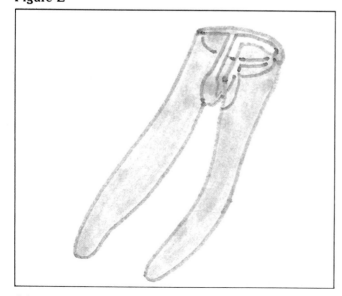

2. Enlarge the head pattern given in **Figure B** to full size. Cut the full-size head out of heavy cardboard.

3. Glue a layer of fiberfill around the raw edges of the cardboard body, as shown in **Figure C.**

4. Force the base of the cardboard head into the slot cut in the wooden dowel rod, and glue it in place. Wrap package tape tightly around the dowel rod below the head to provide extra support **(Figure D).**

5. Cut 1 leg from the pantyhose, eliminating the waistline and center seams as illustrated in **Figure E.**

6. Gather the leg in your hands up to the toe (as if you were going to put it on) and ease the hose leg over the cardboard nose. Stretch the hose over the head, positioning the toe seam at the mouth and the leg opening around the dowel rod.

7. Stuff 1 side of the head using a handful of fiberfill at a time. Work from the tip of the nose to the opening. Repeat the stuffing procedure for the remaining side of the head.

8. Gather the open end of the hose using a needle and heavy-duty thread. Pull the thread to close the opening around the dowel rod, and lock the stitches. Trim the hose to 3 inches long.

9. Tie a red bow over the gathers at the bottom of the head.

Forming the ears, eyes, nose, and mouth

1. Cut two 4-inch-diameter circles from the remaining hose leg.

Figure F	Figure G	Figure H
	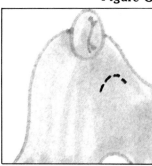	

2. Gently stretch 1 hose circle around a 3-inch-diameter ball of fiberfill to form an ear. Crease 1 side with your finger and gently pull the top of the ear to form a point **(Figure F)**. Tie the raw edges together with thread.

3. Whipstitch the ears to the top of the head, hiding the raw edges.

4. Draw 2 equally spaced half-circles on either side of the face, 3 inches down from the ears **(Figure G).**

5. Pinch up a ridge under each of the half-circles and stitch back and forth under the ridge with heavy-duty thread to shape an eyelid. Take 1 long stitch beneath the eyelid to pull the opposite ends together in a gentle curve. Lock the stitch.

6. Sew white buttons beneath the eyelids. Draw black pupils in the center of each button using a laundry marker.

7. To form the nostrils, repeat the eyelid process (steps 5 and 6) on either side of the muzzle.

8. Push the end of the muzzle inward and stitch across the indentation to form the mouth **(Figure H).**

9. Spray the completed head with a coat of clear acrylic spray. Let the head dry overnight.

Finishing

1. Cut an entire skein of black yarn into 18-inch lengths for the mane. Center them across a 10-inch strip of black seam binding **(Figure I)**. Machine stitch carefully down the center, through the yarn and seam binding.

2. Hand stitch the mane to the head, beginning just in front of the ears.

3. Use the striped grosgrain ribbon to form the bridle. Cut a length of ribbon to fit around the muzzle just above the nostrils. Stitch the ribbon together under the chin **(Figure J)**.

4. Cut a 40-inch length of ribbon. Tie the ends of the ribbon to the sides of the muzzle ribbon, leaving 3 inches free. Fold the 3-inch ends inside the mouth and stitch them in place **(Figure K)**.

5. Cut a 30-inch length of ribbon. Wrap the ribbon under the neck and tie it in a bow on the top of the head.

6. Hand tack the long bridle ribbon to the neck ribbon **(Figure L)**.

Figure I

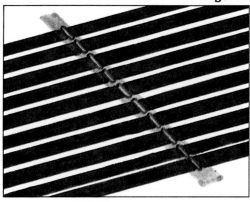

Figure J

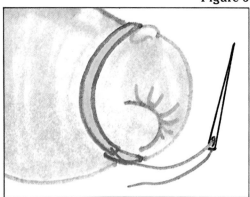

Figure K	Figure L
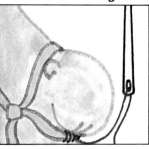	

Picture Frames

You can create a frilly frame for a cherished family picture using opaque knee-high hose and eyelet trim. It's a very personal present to give to grand-parents, or a treasured keepsake for yourself.

Materials

20-inch square of double-thickness mounting board (available at art or drafting supply stores).
1 yard of pre-gathered white eyelet trim.
3 yards of narrow white grosgrain ribbon.
3 pairs of opaque wine-colored knee-high hose.
Small amount of polyester fiberfill.
Razor knife, glue, spring-type clothespins, scissors, straight pins, toothpicks, and a metal ruler.
Paper and pencil to enlarge the patterns.

Cutting the frame pieces

1. Enlarge the frame patterns given in **Figure A** to full size. Use a razor knife to cut the following pieces from double-thickness mounting board: 1 Back, 1 Front, 1 Stand, 2 Vertical Spacers, and 1 Horizontal Spacer. Cut very carefully to keep the edges as straight and even as possible.

2. Score the Stand along the fold line marked on the pattern.

3. Cut the toe seam and the ribbed top from 2 wine-colored hose. Cut each of the hose in half lengthwise so you have 4 pieces. Two of the pieces will be used to cover the sides of the frame. Cut a third piece in half horizontally to cover the top and bottom of the frame.

4. Place 1 side hose piece over the front of the frame, overlapping the opening 1-inch as shown in **Figure B**.

5. Clip the hose along the inside edges of the frame. Fold and glue the center portion of the hose (between the 2 clips) to the wrong side of the frame (**Figure C**).

6. Lift the hose gently and glue a smooth layer of polyester fiberfill to the cardboard frame.

7. Replace the hose over the polyester fiberfill and stretch it around to the back, folding the bottom edge of the hose to a 45-degree angle at the corner as shown in **Figure D**. Wrap and glue the outside edges of the hose to the back of the frame. Use clothespins to hold the hose in place until the glue dries.

8. Repeat steps 1 through 7 to cover the remaining 3 sides of the frame. Use the remaining long hose on the right side and the shorter hose pieces at the top and bottom. Rather than folding the hose at the top left corner, gather it together and tie it with thread to form a flower (**Figure E**).

9. Tie the white grosgrain ribbon in a knot around the gathered flower. Wrap the ribbon at an angle around the entire frame. As you work, gently pull the ribbon to produce a sculptured effect. To end, tie the ribbon in a knot around the gathers.

Figure A

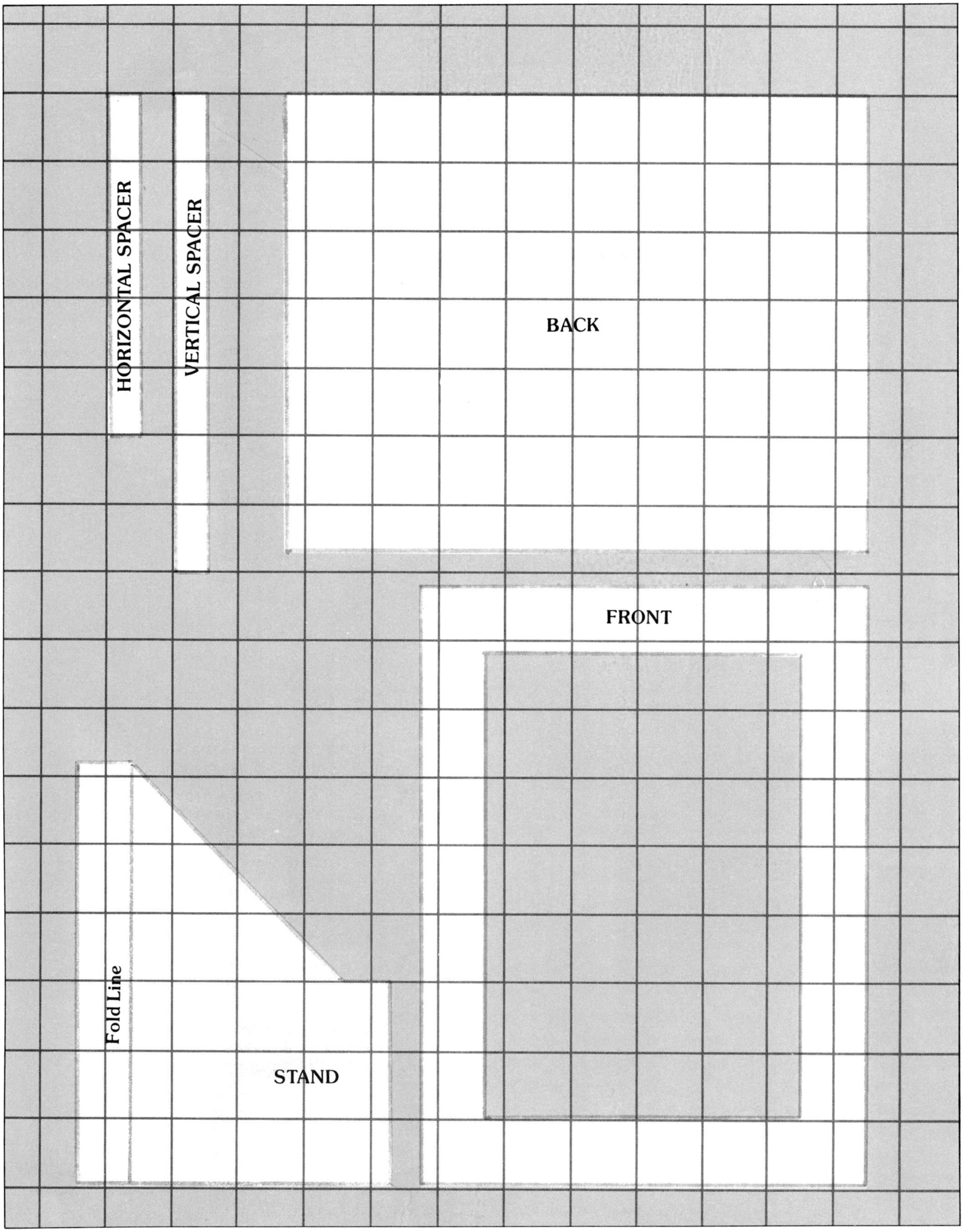

HORIZONTAL SPACER

VERTICAL SPACER

BACK

FRONT

Fold Line

STAND

Figure D

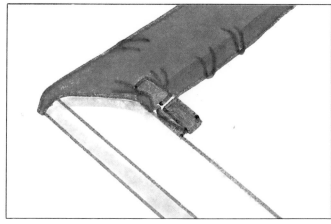

Figure E

Figure B

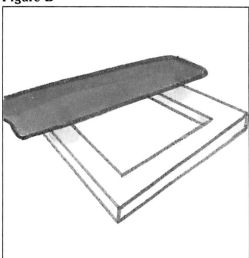

Figure C

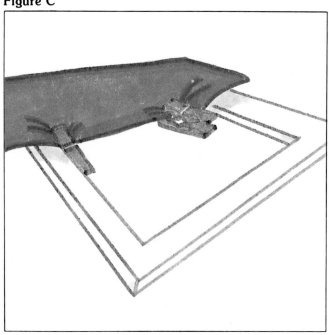

Covering the frame back

1. Cut the ribbed top and the toe seam from 2 additional wine knee-high hose. Cut along 1 side of each hose and open it out flat.

2. Place the 2 flat pieces together and sew a ⅜-inch seam around 3 sides, leaving 1 narrow end open **(Figure F)**. Turn the stitched hose right side out.

3. Wipe glue on the frame Back and spread a thin layer of polyester fiberfill over the glue. Let the glue dry.

4. Stretch the stitched hose over the padded back. Turn the raw edges of the hose to the inside and whipstitch the opening closed.

Covering the stand

1. Cut the ribbed top and the toe seam from 2 knee-high hose. Cut along 1 side of each hose and open it out flat.

2. Place the cardboard stand on top of the 2 flat hose pieces and trace the stand pattern. Cut 2 hose pieces ⅜ inch outside of the traced pattern.

3. Using the traced pattern as a stitching guide, sew the 2 hose pieces together, leaving the longest straight side open and unstitched **(Figure G)**. Turn the stitched hose piece right side out.

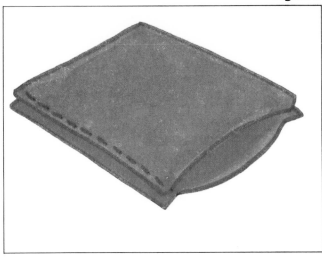

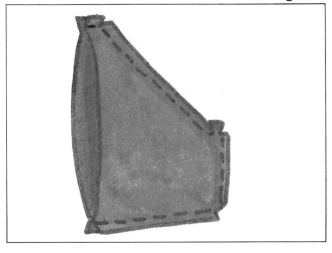

4. Stretch the hose over the cardboard stand. Fold the raw edges of the hose to the inside and whipstitch the opening closed.

5. Bend the completed stand along the fold line. Wipe a generous amount of glue along the folded portion and glue the stand to the back of the frame as shown in **Figure H.**

Assembly

1. Wipe glue on 1 side of each of the spacers and position them ¼ inch from the outside edges on the back of the frame **(Figure I).**

2. Glue the frame front over the spacers. Hold the frame together with clothespins until the glue dries.

3. Use a toothpick to carefully spread glue between the front and back of the assembled frame. Carefully insert the eyelet trim between the glued eyes. Begin at the center bottom and work all the way around the frame. Allow a generous amount of eyelet trim at each of the corners so that the eyelet will turn the corner without pulling. Let the glue dry.

4. Slip your picture inside the frame through the space at the bottom.

Figure I

Ribbon Comb

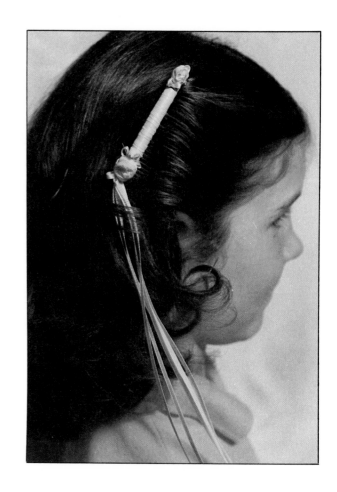

A delightful present for a little girl that is inexpensive and quick to make. She'll want a whole wardrobe of new hair combs in lots of different colors.

Materials

1 hair comb.
2 yards of tiny white satin ribbon.
1 yard of tiny green satin ribbon.
½ yard of tiny pink satin ribbon.
Scraps of nurse's white pantyhose.
White sewing thread and a needle.
Scissors, powdered cheek blusher, and a red felt-tip marker.

Wrapping the comb

1. Hold 2 inches of white ribbon on the back of the comb, and begin wrapping at 1 end. Wrap through each of the spaces between the individual teeth, as shown in **Figure A.**

2. When you reach the end of the comb, tack the white ribbon on the back of the comb to hold it in place.

3. Cut the ribbon, leaving a 14 inches loose on the end.

4. Cut four 12-inch lengths of ribbon for streamers: 1 pink, 2 green, and 1 white. Gather the 4 ends together, and tack them on the back of the comb where you tacked the white ribbon. Pull all 4 ribbons to the front and tack them again **(Figure B).**

Figure A

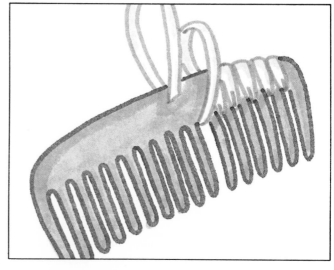

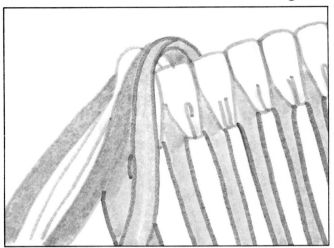

Figure C

Adding the flowers

1. Make 2 loops of green satin ribbon, and tack them over the ribbon streamers at the end of the comb **(Figure C)**.

2. Make 2 additional green satin loops, and tack them to the comb ½-inch from the first loops.

3. To form the large flower, cut a piece of white pantyhose ½ x 1 inch. Fold the hose rectangle in half lengthwise, and follow the illustrations given in **Figure D** to form the flower.

> **a.** Fold over the end of the hose rectangle to form a point.
>
> **b.** Roll the remainder of the rectangle around the point.
>
> **c.** Fold over the free end of the rectangle.
>
> **d.** Stitch the raw edges of the roll together at the bottom.
>
> **e.** Clip off the excess hose below the stitching.

4. Hand tack the stitched bottom of the flower between the green satin loops. Pull the outside edges of the flower out and down, and stitch them to the ribbon, as shown in **Figure E.** This will open out the flower and cover the ends of the green satin ribbon leaves.

5. To form a bud, wrap only once around the folded point. The bud is attached to the ribbon in the same manner as the flower.

6. Make a smaller flower and 3 satin leaves at the other end of the comb.

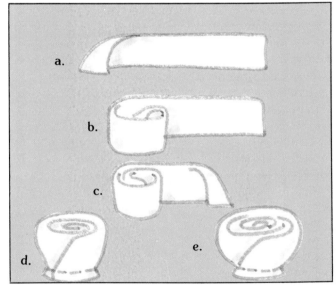

Finishing

1. To color the finished flowers, tip the edges of each flower very lightly using a red felt-tip marker.

2. Brush powdered cheek blusher over the top of each flower.

3. Trim the ribbon streamers to irregular lengths.

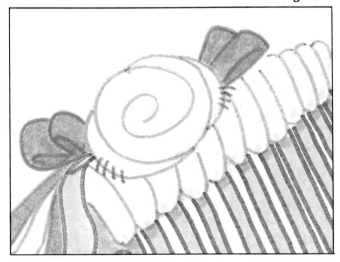

"I Love You" Pillow

A very personal message for the one you love to mark a special occasion, or (best of all) for absolutely no reason.

Materials

½ yard of pink-and-white gingham fabric.
16-inch square of white cotton interfacing fabric.
1 leg of nurse's white pantyhose.
1 yard of 1-inch-wide white eyelet trim.
2 yards of 2-inch-wide white eyelet trim.
½ yard of pink-and-white print ribbon.
14-inch square polyester pillow filler.
12-inch white zipper.
White sewing thread and a needle.
Small amount of polyester fiberfill.
Tracing paper, carbon paper, and a pencil.
Powdered cheek blusher and a red felt-tip marker.

Making the heart

1. A full-size pattern for the heart and message in the center of the pillow is provided in **Figure A.** Use tracing paper and a pencil to trace it, and transfer it to the center of the 16-inch square piece of white cotton interfacing using carbon paper.

2. Cut a piece of white pantyhose slightly larger than the heart pattern. Pin the hose piece over the heart pattern in the center of the interfacing so it overlaps the traced lines. Stitch the hose to the interfacing, sewing over the traced lines.

3. Cut a 16-inch square of pink gingham fabric. Trace the same heart pattern on the wrong side of the gingham, centering it on the square. Cut out the center of the traced heart, leaving a 1-inch border inside the line. Clip the border with scissors to the line, and press the clipped border to the wrong side **(Figure B).**

4. Place the gingham (wrong side down) on top of the hose so that the 2 heart patterns are aligned. Whipstitch the pressed edge of the gingham over the stitched edge of the hose as shown in **Figure C.**

I Love You!

Figure B

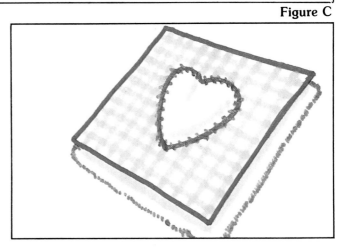

Figure C

Figure D

Figure E

Figure F

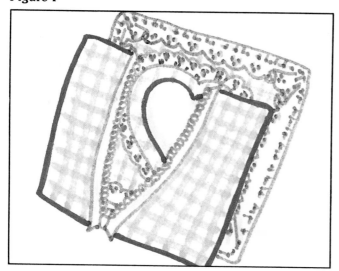

5. Leaving a ½-inch-wide border of gingham showing, stitch the 1-inch-wide white eyelet around the heart, beginning and ending at the top center of the heart (**Figure D**).

6. Slit the back of the interfacing behind the hose heart, and stuff the heart evenly with polyester fiberfill. Add only a small amount of fiberfill at a time. When the heart is completely stuffed, whipstitch the opening in the interfacing together.

Sewing the pillow

1. Cut a 17 x 16-inch gingham rectangle. Fold the rectangle along the 17-inch side and cut along the fold to form 2 pieces, each 8½ x 16 inches.

2. Install the zipper (as directed on the package) between the two 16-inch edges, and press the seams open (**Figure E**).

3. Place the finished pillow front right side up on a flat surface.

4. Pin the 2-inch eyelet trim ½-inch from the edge around the outside of the pillow front, with the ruffle facing in toward the center and the bound edge facing out. Allow a very generous amount of trim at all 4 corners of the pillow. When the pillow is turned right side out, the trim will require enough fullness to turn the corners. Begin and end the trim at the bottom center of the pillow.

5. Topstitch the eyelet trim to the pillow front.

6. Place the fabric back (right side down and with the zipper open) on top of the pillow front. (The trim will be between the front and back.) Stitch around the outside edges, through all 3 layers (**Figure F**).

7. Trim all the edges to ⅜ inch and clip the corners.

8. Turn the pillow right side out and press it with a steam iron. Insert the pillow filler, and zip up the back.

Finishing

1. Full-size lettering is given in Figure A which you can transfer to the heart with carbon paper; however, it is much more personal if you write it in your own handwriting. Whichever way you choose, write it across the center of the heart using a permanent red felt-tip marker.

2. Brush powdered cheek blusher around the outer portions of the heart.

3. Tie the pink print ribbon in a bow, and tack it to the top of the heart.

Grandmother's Keepsake

A beautiful and very personal gift for a grandmother to thank her for all the cookies she's baked and the love with which she serves them.

Figure A

Materials

1 leg cut from a pair of regular pantyhose.
2 yards of 1-inch-wide pre-gathered lace trim.
1 yard of blue, pink, and white calico.
1 yard of white cotton interfacing facing.
18 x 24-inch artist's canvas board.
18 x 24-inch piece of lightweight cardboard.
1 yard of eyelet lace (slotted for ribbon).
5 yards of narrow blue ribbon.
5 yards of narrow pink ribbon.
White beads.
2 yards of ½-inch-wide pink grosgrain ribbon.
2 yards of ½-inch-wide blue grosgrain ribbon.
1 yard of polyester quilt batting.
Light blue acrylic paint and a small paint brush.
Glue, scissors, white sewing thread, and a needle.
Heavy-duty thread and a long sharp needle.
Sawtooth picture hanger, and a permanent black laundry marker.
Paper and pencil to enlarge the pattern.
Tracing paper, carbon paper, and package tape.
¼ pound of polyester fiberfill.

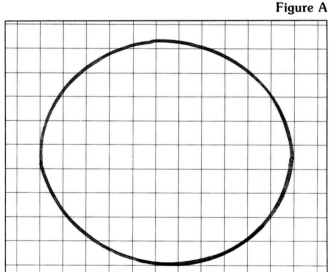

Making the board

1. Enlarge the pattern for the center oval given in **Figure A** to full size.

25

Figure E

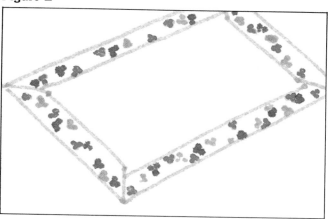

Figure B

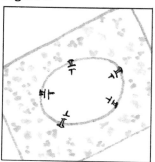

Figure C

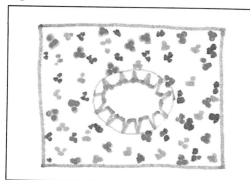

Figure D

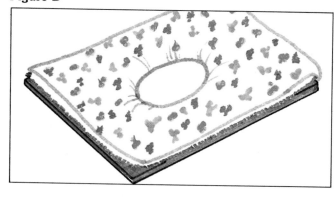

5. Pull the calico fabric through the oval to turn it right side out, and press the stitched seam.

6. Cut a 28 x 24-inch rectangle of polyester quilt batting. Center the oval pattern on the batting and trace it with a pencil. Cut out the center of the traced oval.

7. Lift the edges of the calico border, and slip them through the oval in the batting. Position the batting between the calico and interfacing.

8. Place the assembled border over the 18 x 24-inch canvas board, centering the oval. Glue the edges of the oval to the canvas board **(Figure D)**.

9. Wrap the edges of the border to the back side of the canvas board and tape them in place with strong packing tape. Miter each of the 4 corners, as shown in **Figure E**.

10. Glue the 18 x 14-inch piece of lightweight cardboard over the back of the canvas board to cover the edges of the fabric.

11. Attach a sawtooth picture hanger to the back of the canvas board.

12. Thread narrow pink and blue satin ribbon through the slots in the 1-inch-wide lace. Glue the lace to the edge of the oval cutout, beginning and ending at the center bottom. Gather the lace slightly to curve gently around the oval.

13. Cut and glue the ends of the lace together at the center bottom. Let the glue dry, and tie a bow in both the pink and blue ribbons to cover the lace ends.

Adding the lettering

1. Full-size lettering for the center is provided in **Figure F.** Trace the lettering and use carbon paper to transfer it to the canvas board, centering it inside the oval.

2. Paint the transferred lettering with blue acrylic paint using a small paint brush. Let the paint dry overnight.

Making the grandchildren

1. To make 1 baby face, form a 1-inch-diameter ball of polyester fiberfill. Cover the fiberfill with a 3-inch-diameter circle cut from regular pantyhose. Tie the raw edges of the hose together in the back.

2. Center the full-size pattern on the wrong side of the calico fabric and pin it in place **(Figure B).** Trace the outside of the pattern with a pencil.

3. Stitch the calico and white cotton interfacing wrong sides together, using the traced oval as the stitching line.

4. Cut out the center of the stitched oval, leaving a 1-inch-wide seam allowance around the inside. Clip the seam allowance **(Figure C).**

Grandma is someone who treats you the best and grumbles the least.

Figure G

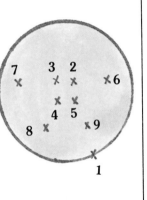

Figure H

2.   Follow the entry and exit points illustrated in **Figure G** to form the baby's facial features. Use a long sharp needle and heavy-duty thread.

    a.   Enter at 1 and exit at 2. Sew a tiny circle of basting stitches in the center of the face, exiting at 3.

    b.   Use the tip of the needle to very slightly lift the fiberfill within the circle. Gently pull the thread until a small round nose appears.

    c.   Hold the thread with 1 hand and lock the stitch under the bridge of the nose, exiting at 2.

    d.   To form the nostrils, reenter at 2 and exit at 4.

    e.   Reenter at 4 and exit at 3.

    f.   Reenter at 3 and exit at 5.

    g.   Reenter at 5 and exit at 2. Lock the stitch under the bridge of the nose.

    h.   To form the eyes, enter at 2 and exit at 6.

    i.   Pull the thread over the surface, enter at 2 and exit at 3.

    j.   Reenter at 3 and exit at 7.

    k.   Pull the thread over the surface, enter at 3 and exit at 2. Gently pull the thread until closed eyes appear, and lock the stitch.

    l.   To form the mouth, enter at 2 and exit at 8.

    m.   Pull the thread across the surface, enter at 9 and exit at 3. Pull the thread until the smile appears.

    n.   Reenter at 3 and exit at 1. Lock the stitch and cut the thread.

3.   Repeat steps 1 and 2 to make as many baby faces as there are grandchildren in the family.

Assembly

1.   Arrange the baby faces on top of the calico border, placing them evenly around the oval. When you have the arrangement you want, cut a small hole through the border (calico, polyester, and interfacing) where each of the faces should be positioned. Glue the knot on each of the baby faces directly to the canvas board. This will prevent the border from sagging from the weight of the baby heads when the picture is complete.

2.   After the glue has dried, measure and cut lace to fit around each of the babies' heads. Glue it in place, as shown in **Figure H.**

Figure I

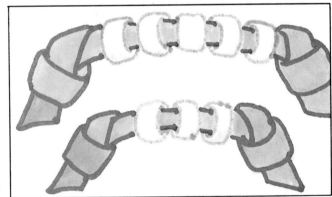

3.   Each of the grandchildren's names and birthdates are printed on white beads under the baby faces. Each baby requires 2 ribbons threaded with beads. Choose pink ribbons for the girls and blue for the boys. Knot 1 end of the ribbon and thread 1 bead over the ribbon for each letter in the child's name. Knot the other end of the ribbon, and cut it off. Glue the ribbon underneath the baby's face.

4.   Knot another ribbon and thread 3 beads (for the birthdate). Knot the ribbon again and cut it off. Glue the birthdate ribbon underneath the name ribbon **(Figure I).**

5.   Repeat steps 3 and 4 for each of the faces.

6.   Print the child's name and birthdate on the white beads using a permanent black laundry marker.

27

Little Black Evening Bag

If you've always admired the evening purses in the stores but hated to spend the money, then this project is for you! Stitch it up in your choice of colors and trims.

Materials

1 pair of black opaque knee-high hose.
Panty portion cut from a pair of nurse's white pantyhose.
1 yard of gold elastic cord.
1 yard of black grosgrain ribbon.
1 yard of gold glitter trim.
1 yard of black satin cording.
10-inch-long spring-type metal purse closure.
Heavy-duty black thread, and a long sharp needle.
Polyester quilt batting and scissors.

Making the purse

1. Cut off the ribbed top and the toe seam on 2 black knee-high hose. Cut along 1 side and open each hose out flat.

2. Cut 2 rectangular pieces from the panty portion of a pair of white hose to match the size of the black hose pieces, avoiding the seams in the panty **(Figure A)**.

3. Place the 2 black hose pieces together and stitch along both short sides and across the bottom, as shown in **Figure B**.

4. Turn the stitched black hose right side out. This will be the outside of the purse.

5. Sew the 2 white hose pieces together along the bottom seam only.

Figure A

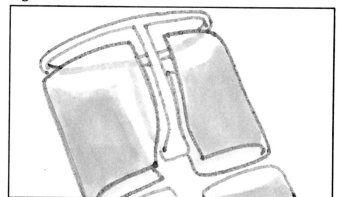

Figure B

Figure C

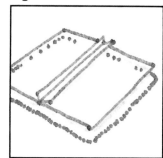

28

Figure D

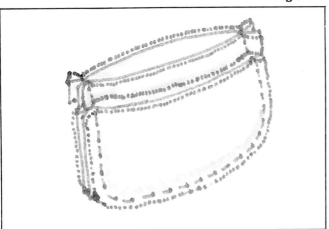

Figure E

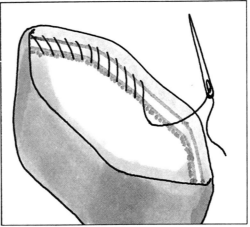

Figure F

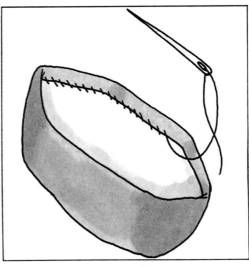

6. Cut a rectangle of batting the size of the stitched white hose as shown in **Figure C**. Baste the batting and white hose together on all 4 edges, placing the stitched hose seam on the inside.

7. Fold the white hose together so the batting is on the outside. Stitch the side seams together, and trim off 1 inch along both the top edges (**Figure D**).

8. Slip the white hose lining with attached batting inside the black purse.

9. Insert the spring-type metal purse closure inside the purse even with the top of the lining, and baste in place (**Figure E**).

10. Wrap the black hose over the metal closure and whipstitch it to the lining, turning the edges of the black hose under (**Figure F**).

11. Use heavy-duty black thread to stitch through all the layers underneath the closure to hold it firmly in place (**Figure G**).

12. To section the purse with gold cord, follow the entry and exit points illustrated in **Figure H**.

    a. Knot the cord and enter on the inside of the purse behind 1. Exit at 1.

    b. Wrap the cord completely around the outside of the purse and enter at 2. Lock the stitch without pulling the cord, and cut the thread.

    c. Repeat the procedure 1 more time — between points 3 and 4, locking the stitch after the wrap.

Finishing

1. Cut the black silk cord to the proper length to fit over your shoulder, and hand tack the ends inside the purse.

2. Stitch black grosgrain ribbon inside the purse around the top edges to cover the knotted gold cord and the ends of the shoulder cord (**Figure I**).

3. Cut two 2-inch lengths of gold trim. Fold them in half to form tabs and securely stitch them to the center top of the purse on the outside (**Figure J**).

4. Whipstitch gold glitter trim around the outside of the purse over the metal closure at the top.

Figure G

Figure H

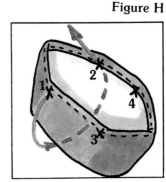

Figure I

Figure J

Ski Vest & Hat

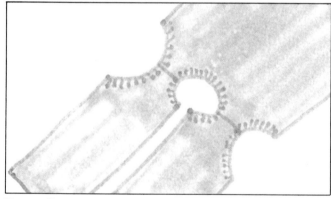

You can recycle a worn sweater vest into a great looking "down" ski vest. Add a matching hat, and you're off to the slopes!

Figure A

Figure B

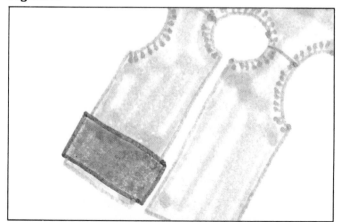

Materials

For the vest:
>V-neck sweater vest, the back of which is in good condition.
>Knee-high opaque hose in 3 different colors: 3 pairs of black, 1 pair of wine, and 1 pair of brown.
>2 yards of wine grosgrain ribbon.
>¼ pound of polyester fiberfill.

For the hat:
>5 legs of knee-high opaque hose: 2 wine, 2 black and 1 blue.
>Polyester fiberfill.

Scissors, straight pins, needle and sewing thread.

Making the vest

1. Cut the sweater vest from the neckline to the bottom down the center front. Cut the side seams open and lay the vest on a flat surface **(Figure A)**.

2. Cut the ribbed top and the toe seam from 4 knee-high hose: 2 black, 1 wine, and 1 brown. Cut along 1 side of the hose and open each of them out flat.

3. Place the brown hose piece on top of the vest at the bottom left. Trim the piece so that it overlaps the center and side of the vest ½ inch **(Figure B)**. Pin it in place.

Figure C

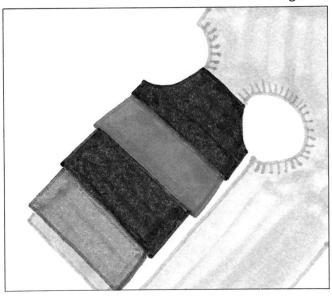

4. Place a black hose piece above the brown one, overlapping the pieces ½ inch.

5. Place a wine hose piece above the black, again overlapping the edges.

6. Place a second black hose piece over the wine hose, trimming it to fit around the armhole and the neckline as shown in **Figure C.**

7. Remove the 4 pieces from the vest, and stitch them together along their overlapping edges **(Figure D).**

8. Replace the assembled vest side on top of the sweater vest. Turn the raw edges of the hose under along the shoulder seam and around the armhole. Whipstitch it in place.

9. Cut a double layer of polyester fiberfill the size of the stitched hose, and sandwich it between the hose and the sweater **(Figure E).** Baste around the edges of the vest to secure the layers together.

10. Topstitch over each of the seam lines between the contrasting hose pieces.

11. Repeat steps 2 through 10 to complete the remaining vest side.

Finishing

1. Cut 2-inch-wide strips from the remaining black knee-high hose. Stitch the strips together, end to end, to form 1 continuous trim piece.

2. Pin the trim piece over the bottom edges and around the neck, as shown in **Figure F.** Miter the corners, and stitch ½ inch from the edge.

3. Fold the trim piece around the edge, turn the raw edges under and whipstitch the trim on the inside **(Figure G).**

4. Cut the 2 yards of wine ribbon into 6 equal pieces. Stitch each of the pieces inside the front opening even with each of the stitched seams in the vest **(Figure H).**

5. Pin the vest right sides together at the side seams, and stitch them together securely. Turn it right side out.

Figure D

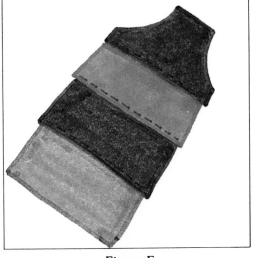

Figure E

Figure F

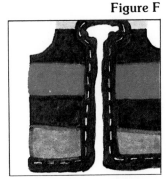

Figure G

Figure H

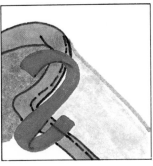

Figure K

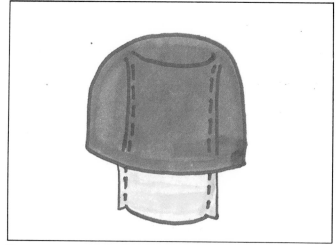

Figure L

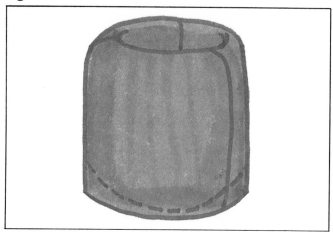

Figure I

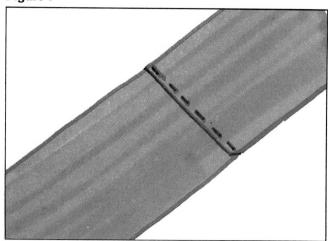

Figure J

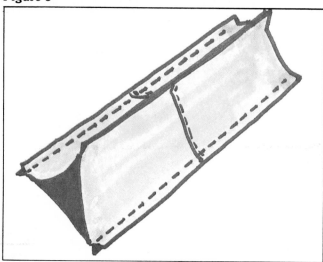

Making the hat

1. Cut the ribbed top and the toe seam from 5 legs of knee-high hose (2 wine, 2 black, and 1 blue). Cut along 1 side and open each hose flat.

2. Place the narrow end of the 2 wine hose pieces together and stitch **(Figure I)**. Repeat for the 2 black hose pieces.

3. Cut the remaining blue hose piece in half lengthwise. Stitch the narrow end of the 2 hose halves together.

4. Stitch the 3 long hose pieces eight sides together as shown in **Figure J.** Then stitch the end panels together to form a tube.

5. Fold the tube in half, turning it back over itself so the stitched seams are on the inside and the raw edges are together **(Figure K).**

6. Slip a double layer of polyester batting between the 2 hose layers, working through the opening between the 2 raw edges.

7. Flatten the tube and stitch a curve across the raw edges, as shown in **Figure L.** Trim off the excess seam.

8. Turn the hat right side out, and turn up the cuff all the way around.

KID STUFF

... for that special child

Child's Keepsake Picture

If your child has a favorite item of clothing that is outgrown but too much of a treasure to part with, here's the answer! We used a much-loved Cub Scout uniform, but the same project could be made with a Brownie uniform or any special shirt.

Materials

12-inch-square piece of blue felt (or a Cub Scout shirt).
1 pantyhose leg.
Small amount of polyester fiberfill.
Heavy-duty nylon thread and a long sharp needle.
Small amount of yellow fiber.
12 x 18-inch piece of yellow felt.
12 x 18-inch piece of heavy cardboard.
Cub Scout hat, tie, tie slide, and awards.
12 x 18-inch picture frame.
Powdered cheek blusher and brown felt-tip marker.
Scissors and glue.

Constructing the background

1. Wipe a thin layer of glue on the 12 x 18-inch piece of heavy cardboard and cover it with the matching piece of yellow felt. Allow the glue to dry.

2. (If you are using an actual shirt, skip this step and go to step 3.) Enlarge the shirt pattern given in **Figure A** to full size and cut it out of blue felt.

3. Glue the shirt to the lower portion of the background. If you have used an actual shirt and do not wish to cut it, wrap the excess around to the back of the cardboard **(Figure B)**.

4. Wrap the Cub Scout tie around the neckline of the shirt and slip the tie slide over the tie ends. Wrap the tie ends around the back of the cardboard.

5. Glue any awards you may have to the background, as shown in the photograph.

Figure A

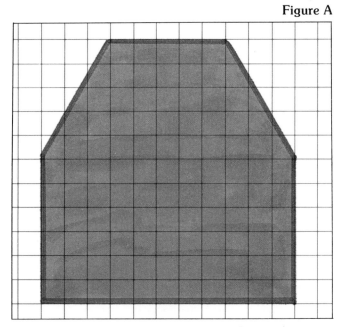

Figure B

Figure C

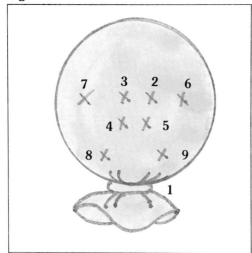

Figure D

Making the face

1. Cut a 12-inch section of pantyhose leg. Tie a knot in 1 end and turn the hose inside out so the knot is on the inside.

2. Stuff the hose with generous amounts of fiberfill until the head is sized to the hat and about 3 inches thick. Tie the hose in a knot at the "neck."

3. Follow the entry and exit points illustrated in **Figure C** to form the facial features. Use a long sharp needle and 1 long heavy-duty thread for the entire procedure.

    a. Enter at 1 and exit at 2. Sew a circle of basting stitches approximately 2 inches in diameter, exiting at 3.

    b. Use the tip of the needle to very carefully lift the fiberfill within the circle just enough to make a small bulge. Gently pull the thread until a small round nose appears.

    c. Hold the thread with 1 hand and lock the stitch under the bridge of the nose, exiting at 2.

    d. To form the nostrils, reenter at 2 and exit at 4.

    e. Reenter ¼ inch directly above 4 and exit at 3.

    f. Reenter at 3 and exit at 5.

    g. Reenter ¼ inch directly above 5 and exit at 2. Lock the stitch under the bridge of the nose.

    h. To form the eyes, enter at 2 and exit at 6.

    i. Pull the thread over the surface, enter at 2 and exit at 3.

    j. Reenter at 3 and exit at 7.

    k. Pull the thread across the surface, enter at 3 and exit at 2. Gently pull the thread until closed eyes appear, and lock the stitch.

    l. To form the mouth, enter at 2 and exit at 8.

    m. Pull the thread across the surface, enter at 9 and exit at 3. Pull the thread until the smile appears.

    n. Reenter at 3 and exit at 1. Lock the stitch and cut the thread.

    o. The bottom lip is formed by repeating the last 3 steps (1 through n) just under the mouth line using a smaller stitch.

4. Brush powdered cheek blushers on cheeks and bottom lip. Dot freckles across the nose and cheeks with a narrow felt-tip marker.

Finishing

1. Glue the head in position at the shirt neckline, hiding the gathers between the head and the background.

2. Glue strands of fiber at the top of the head, and spread them across the forehead.

3. Fold the back half of the cap inside the front half and place it over the top of the head **(Figure D).** Stitch and glue the cap to the background. Take several stitches completely through the felt and cardboard to make sure the finished picture will not pull loose.

4. Frame the completed picture as you would any other.

Toddler Toys

Little Brown Bear and Little Gray Mouse are perfect toys for toddlers. Inside their soft bodies are egg-shaped pantyhose containers that hold a bell – so they rattle and jingle when shaken.

Materials

To make 1 toy:

1 pair of heavy "winter" hose: dark brown for the bear; gray for the mouse.

½ yard of satin ribbon: yellow for the bear; pink for the mouse.

Empty egg-shaped pantyhose container and a bell.

Pink and black cotton embroidery thread, and an embroidery needle.

Heavy-duty thread and a long sharp needle.

Polyester fiberfill, scissors, and string.

Making the body

1. Tie a knot in 1 leg of pantyhose at the panty line. Cut 4 inches above the knot. Cut again 4 inches above the toe seam **(Figure A).** Turn the hose so the knot is inside.

2. Stuff the lower 4 inches of the hose with polyester fiberfill. Form a cavity in the center of the fiberfill.

Figure A

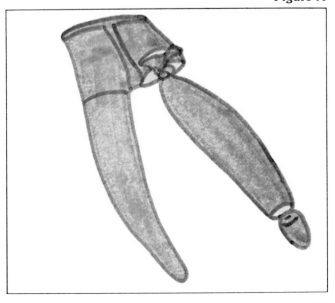

Figure E

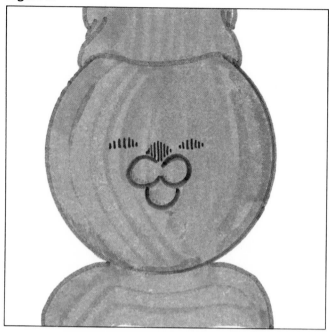

Figure B

Figure C

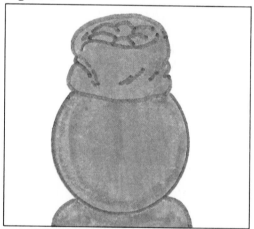

Figure D

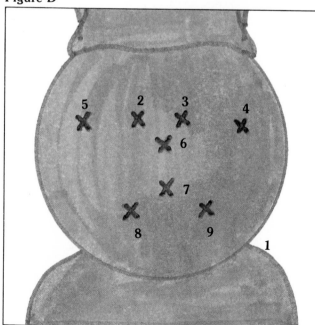

3. Put the bell inside the egg-shaped container and glue the container halves together. Place the container inside the cavity in the fiberfill, and continue stuffing the hose body to within 6 inches of the top opening. Tie the hose in a knot.

4. Separate the body from the head by tying a string around the neck, 6 inches from the bottom **(Figure B).**

5. Fold the hose down over the knot at the top of the head to form the hat **(Figure C).** Turn the raw edges under and whipstitch them to the head.

Stitching the Little Brown Bear

1. Use a needle and heavy-duty thread to form the bear's facial features, following the entry and exit points illustrated in **Figure D.**

    a. Enter at 1 and exit at 2.

    b. Sew a clockwise circle of basting stitches in the center of the face about 1½ inches in diameter, ending at 3. Pull the thread and lock the stitch.

    c. Reenter at 3 and exit at 4.

    d. Enter at 3 and exit at 5.

    e. Enter at 2 and exit at 6. Pull the thread and lock the stitch.

    f. Enter at 3 and exit at 2.

    g. Enter at 6 and exit at 7. Pull the thread and lock the stitch.

    h. Enter at 6 and exit at 8. Pull the thread and lock the stitch.

    i. Enter at 9 and exit at 2. Pull the thread and lock the stitch.

2. Embroider the nose and eyes with the satin stitch using a full strand of black embroidery thread **(Figure E).** Illustrated embroidery stitch instructions are given in the "Tips and Techniques" section at the front of this book.

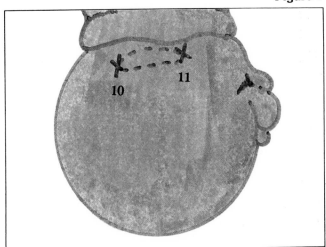

Figure F

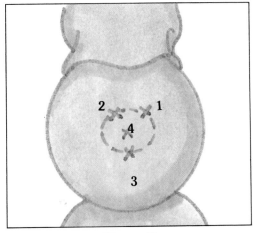

Figure G

3. Embroider the mouth with the satin stitch using a full strand of pink embroidery thread.

4. To form the ears, follow the entry and exit points illustrated in **Figure F.**

    a. Enter at 1 and exit at 10.

    b. Pinch up a horizontal ridge between 10 and 11. Stitch back and forth underneath the ridge, exiting at 11.

    c. Reenter at 11 and exit at 10.

    d. Pull the thread over the top of the ear ridge. Enter at 11 and exit at 10.

    e. Pull the thread tightly and lock the stitch.

5. Repeat the procedure in step 1 on the other side of the hat to form the other ear.

Stitching the Little Gray Mouse

1. To form the mouse's facial features, follow the entry and exit points illustrated in **Figure G.**

    a. Pinch up a vertical ridge in the center of the face. Enter at 1 and exit at 2.

    b. Sew a clockwise circle of basting stitches below the ridge, ending at 2. Pull the thread and lock the stitch.

    c. Pull the thread over the ridge. Enter at 1 and exit at 2.

    d. Pull the thread over the ridge ½ inch lower than the previous stitch. Enter at 1 and exit at 2. Pull the thread and lock the stitch.

    e. Center at 2 and exit at 3.

    f. Enter below the nose at 4 and exit at 2. Pull the thread and lock the stitch.

2. Embroider the mouse's nose with pink embroidery thread and his eyes black using the satin stitch **(Figure H).** Illustrated instructions for embroidery stitches are given in the "Tips and Techniques" section at the beginning of this book.

3. To form the ears, pinch up a large flattened ridge. Follow the same stitching procedure used for the bear's ears ("Stitching the Little Brown Bear" steps 4 and 5).

4. Complete the mouse by embroidering the inside of each stitched ear with pink embroidery thread using the satin stitch **(Figure I).**

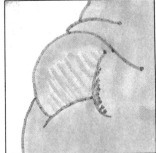

Figure H

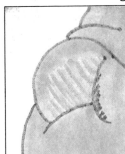

Figure I

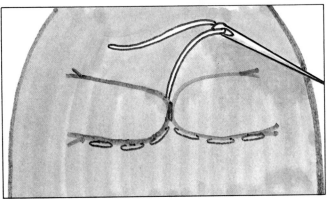

Figure J

Finishing

1. To form the arms, pinch up a ridge across the chest. Stitch back and forth under the ridge, returning to the top center of the ridge.

2. Take a vertical stitch across the ridge and return to the center top. Tighten the thread to separate the arms and lock the stitch **(Figure J).**

3. Repeat steps 1 and 2 at the bottom of the figure to form the legs.

4. Tie a satin bow around the neck.

Birth Record

A wonderfully personal way to mark the exciting event of your own baby's birth, and a beautiful gift for the brand new mother on your list.

Materials

12-inch-diameter wooden embroidery hoop.
2 yards of 1-inch-wide white eyelet trim.
½ yard of blue-and-white striped fabric.
1 yard of narrow blue satin ribbon.
1 leg cut from nurse's white pantyhose.
½ yard of ½-inch-wide white lace.
3 x 4-inch piece of white cotton fabric.
Small amount of polyester fiberfill.
Scrap piece of regular pantyhose.
Heavy-duty white thread, a long sharp needle, and a permanent felt-tip marker.

Making the bassinet

1. Stretch the blue-and-white striped fabric over the embroidery hoop. The stripes should run vertically when the tightening screw is placed at the top of the picture.

2. The bassinet is formed with 3 rows of eyelet trim. Measure and cut 7 inches of eyelet for the bottom tier. Turn the raw ends to the underside and whipstitch the eyelet to the striped fabric. Follow the curves of the hoop and center the eyelet at the bottom (**Figure A**).

3. Cut and stitch 2 more tiers of eyelet trim to overlap the first. Each subsequent trim piece should be slightly shorter than the previous one.

4. To make the hood for the bassinet, form a half-circle of polyester fiberfill with a radius of 2½ inches and a diameter of 5 inches. Cover the fiberfill with a piece of white hose, and stitch the raw edges together on the underside.

Figure A

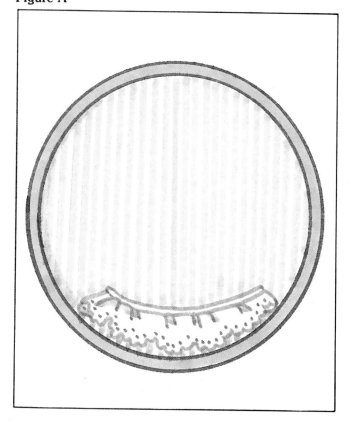

5. Follow the entry and exit points illustrated in **Figure B** to section the hood.

    a. Enter on the underside and exit at 1.

    b. Enter at 2 and exit at 3.

    c. Enter at 4 and exit at 5.

    d. Enter at 6 and exit at 7.

    e. Enter at 8 and exit on the underside. Lock the stitch and cut the thread.

6. Whipstitch eyelet trim over the 5-inch-edge of the hose. Position the assembled bassinet hood over the tiered eyelet and whipstitch it in place **(Figure C).**

7. Tie a blue satin ribbon bow and tack it to the top of the bassinet.

Making the baby

1. Form a 1-inch-diameter ball of polyester fiberfill, and cover it with a 3-inch-diameter circle cut from regular pantyhose. Tie the raw edges of the hose together in the back.

2. Follow the entry and exit points illustrated in **Figure D** to form the baby's facial features. Use a long sharp needle and heavy-duty thread.

    a. Enter at 1 and exit at 2. Sew a tiny circle of basting stitches in the center of the face, exiting at 3.

    b. Use the tip of the needle to very slightly lift the fiberfill within the circle. Gently pull the thread until a small round nose appears.

    c. Hold the thread with 1 hand and lock the stitch under the bridge of the nose, exiting at 2.

    d. To form the nostrils, reenter at 2 and exit at 4.

    e. Reenter at 4 and exit at 3.

    f. Reenter at 3 and exit at 5.

    g. Reenter at 5 and exit at 2. Lock the stitch under the bridge of the nose.

    h. To form the eyes, enter at 2 and exit at 6.

    i. Pull the thread over the surface, enter at 2 and exit at 3.

    j. Reenter at 3 and exit at 7.

    k. Pull the thread over the surface, enter at 3 and exit at 2. Gently pull the thread until closed eyes appear, and lock the stitch.

    l. To form the mouth, enter at 2 and exit at 8.

    m. Pull the thread across the surface, enter at 9 and exit at 3. Pull the thread until the smile appears.

    n. Reenter at 3 and exit at 1. Lock the stitch and cut the thread.

3. Cut the toe section from a leg of white pantyhose 6 inches above the toe seam. Form a 3-inch-long cylinder of polyester fiberfill 1 inch in diameter, and place it inside the toe of the hose.

Figure B

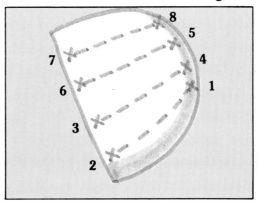

Figure C

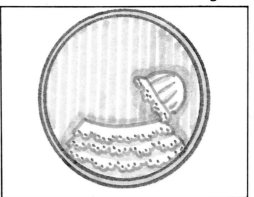

Figure D

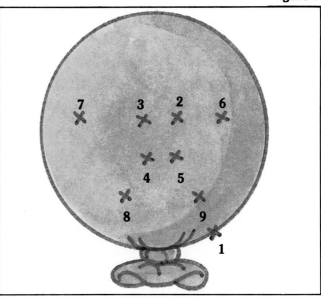

Figure F

Ricky Bartley
Jan 7, 1982
8 lbs 12 oz

4. Turn the raw edges of the hose to the inside and wrap them around the baby's face. Arrange the loose fiberfill to form a body inside the hose, and position the baby head at the top of the bassinet. Wrap the excess hose to the underside, and stitch the assembled baby body to the striped fabric (**Figure E**).

5. Tie a tiny blue satin bow and tack it to the baby's neck.

Finishing

1. Topstitch ½-inch-wide lace around the edges of the 3 x 4-inch white fabric rectangle.

2. Hand letter the baby's name, birthdate, and weight on the fabric rectangle with a permanent felt-tip marker.

3. Hand tack the fabric rectangle above the bassinet.

4. Cut a 12-inch length of blue satin ribbon, and tack the center of it above the lace-trimmed rectangle. Twist the ends of the ribbon and hand tack them to the top corners of the rectangle (**Figure F**).

5. Glue the eyelet trim to the back edge of the hoop. Tie a blue satin bow at the top of the hoop over the tightening screw.

Figure E

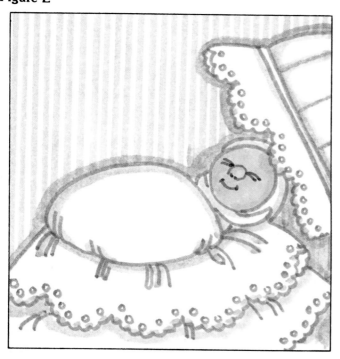

Crib Comforter

A green-and-white gingham cover to wrap your baby snugly on the coldest days – or place on the floor for a cuddly play mat.

Materials

4½ pairs of nurse's white pantyhose.
1 yard of 45-inch-wide green-and-white gingham fabric.
1 yard of 45-inch-wide white cotton interfacing.
Small amount of white yarn and a needle with an *eye* large enough to accommodate 1 strand of yarn.
1½ pounds of polyester fiberfill.
Scissors, white sewing thread, straight pins and a needle.

Making the panels

1. Cut the leg portions from all 4½ pairs of pantyhose, eliminating all seams as illustrated in **Figure A**.

2. Cut each of the 9 hose legs in 3 pieces by cutting the hose in half lengthwise, and then cutting the resulting flat piece in thirds horizontally **(Figure B)**.

Figure A

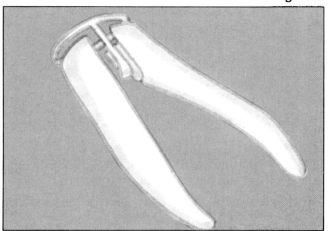

Figure B

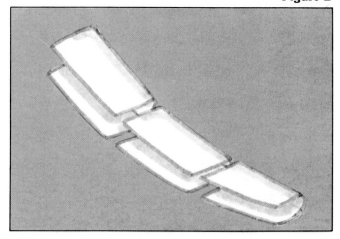

Figure C

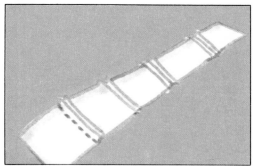

Figure D

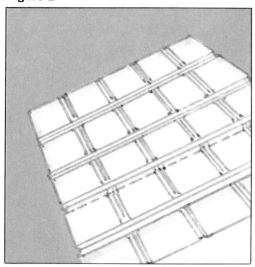

Figure E

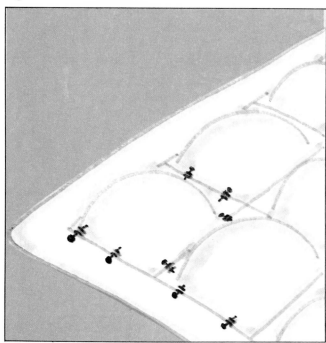

Figure F

Figure G

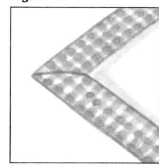

Figure H

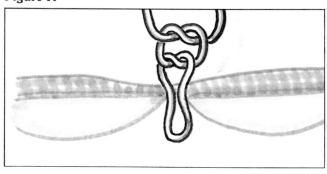

3. Trim 25 of the pieces to a uniform rectangular size. Sew the rectangles, narrow ends together in strips of 5, using a ⅜-inch seam allowance **(Figure C).** Stretch the hose gently as you stitch to retain the elasticity.

4. Sew 5 strips together to make a large rectangle of 25 pieces **(Figure D),** again using a ⅜-inch seam allowance.

5. Trim 2 inches off of each edge of the white cotton interfacing. Place the large hose rectangle right side up on top of the interfacing, leaving an additional 2-inch border of interfacing uncovered. Adjust the seam lines on the large hose rectangle so all 25 panels are equal in size. Pin the seam lines to the interfacing **(Figure E).**

Finishing

1. Cut small openings through the interfacing to correspond with the center of each hose panel.

2. Stuff each hose panel with polyester fiberfill, working through the opening in the interfacing. After stuffing, whipstitch each of the openings closed **(Figure F).**

3. Center the stuffed panel (hose side up) on the wrong side of the gingham fabric. Fold the edges of the gingham over the 2-inch uncovered border of the interfacing and press it flat. Fold the raw edges on the gingham to the underside and whipstitch them in place. Miter the gingham on all 4 corners, as shown in **Figure G.**

4. Thread a large-eye needle with a strand of white yarn. Begin tying at 1 corner of the center hose panel. Take a single stitch through both layers, then tie the yarn on the gingham side in a double knot **(Figure H).**

5. Trim the ends of the knot to about 1 inch in length. Continue tying the corners of the hose panels, working out to all 4 sides.

Ned and Nell

These delightful dolls will be very special additions to your child's doll collection. And they're big enough to wear a child's favorite hand-me-downs!

Materials

To make 2 doll bodies:
    4 pounds of polyester fiberfill.
    3 pairs of pantyhose.
    2 pairs of knee-high hose.
    Heavy-duty thread and a long sharp needle.
    Black felt-tip marker and a sewing machine.
    Paper and pencil to enlarge the patterns.
    Scissors, glue, and straight pins.

For Nell:
    2 ounces of brown fiber.
    12-inch length of 1-inch-wide seam binding.
    1½ yard of 45-inch-wide blue print fabric.
    3 yards of ¼-inch-wide elastic.
    ½-yard of 2-inch-wide flat lace.
    1 hook and eye closure.
    2 yards of 1½-inch-wide eyelet trim.
    Sewing thread to match the fabric.
    1 yard of ¾-inch-wide blue satin ribbon.

For Ned:
    1½ yards of 45-inch-wide denim fabric.
    4 small buttons.
    1 skein of burnt-orange rug yarn.
    Blue and white acrylic paint, and a small paint brush.
    Purchased size 4 boy's shirt.

Figure A

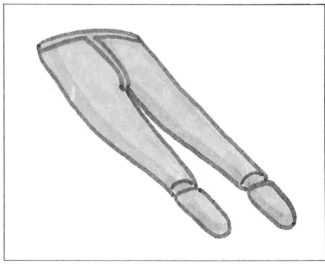

Making the body

1. To make the legs and trunk, turn 1 pair of pantyhose wrong side out. Cut away the bottom 7 inches of each leg **(Figure A)**. Machine stitch across the cut edges and turn the hose right side out.

45

Figure B

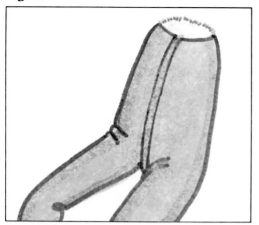

Figure C

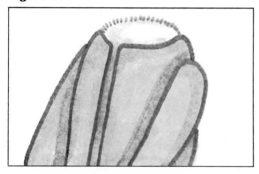

Figure D

Figure E

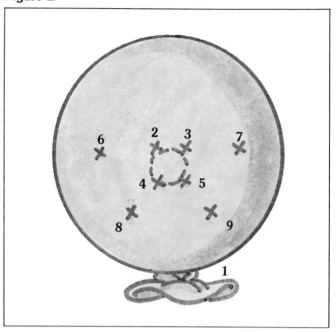

Making the head

1. To form the head, tie a knot at the panty line on 1 leg of pantyhose. Cut 1 inch above the knot. Cut again 10 inches below the knot. Turn the hose so the knot is on the inside.

2. Stuff generous amounts of fiberfill inside the head, manipulating the shape until a head is formed **(Figure D)**. The completed head should measure approximately 20 inches in circumference. Tie the hose in a knot at the neck.

3. Use a long sharp needle and heavy-duty thread to form the nose. Follow the entry and exit points illustrated in **Figure E.**

    a. Enter at 1 and exit at 2. Sew a circle of basting stitches approximately 2 inches in diameter, exiting at 3.

    b. Use the tip of the needle to carefully lift the fiberfill within the circle just enough to make a small bulge. Gently pull the thread until a round nose appears.

    c. Hold the thread with 1 hand and lock the stitch under the bridge of the nose, exiting at 2.

    d. To form the nostrils, reenter at 2 exit at 4.

    e. Reenter ¼ inch above 4 and exit at 3.

    f. Reenter at 3 and exit at 5.

    g. Reenter ¼ inch above 5 and exit at 2. Lock the stitch under the bridge of the nose.

4. Continue working with the same thread to form the mouth.

    a. Enter at 2 and exit at 8.

    b. Pull the thread across the surface, enter at 9 and exit at 3.

    c. Pull the thread until a smile appears. Reenter at 3 and exit at 1.

    d. Lock the stitch and cut the thread.

5. The bottom lip can be produced by repeating step 4 just below the mouth using a smaller stitch. Return to 1 and lock the stitch.

2. Stuff each leg with polyester fiberfill. Work from the toe up and keep the 2 legs equal to each other in size. When finished, the legs should be approximately 19 inches long and 9½ inches in circumference. Continue stuffing the panty portion of the hose to form the trunk of the body **(Figure B)**.

3. Stuff 2 knee-high hose to form the arms. Keep the arms as equal in size as possible. When stuffed, the arms should be approximately 15 inches long and 8 inches in circumference. Tie a knot in the hose at the top of the arm.

4. Position the arms at a slight angle to the shoulders. Use heavy-duty thread and a needle to whipstitch the arms to the body **(Figure C)**.

6. Brush powdered cheek blusher on the cheeks and across the bottom lip. Dot freckles on the nose and cheeks with a narrow felt-tip marker.

7. To form the ears, follow the entry and exit points illustrated in **Figure F.**

    a. Pinch up a small ridge at an angle on the side of the head just below the eye line. Enter at 1 and exit at 9.

    b. Stitch under the ridge back and forth until an ear forms. Exit at 10.

    c. Lock the stitch and return to 1.

    d. Lock the stitch and trim the thread.

8. Repeat step 7 on the other side of the head.

Making Ned's eyes

1. To form Ned's open eyes, follow the entry and exit points illustrated in **Figure G.**

    a. Enter at 2 and exit at 3.

    b. Enter at 4 and exit at 2.

    c. Enter again at 4 and exit at 2.

    d. Enter at 3 and exit at 2.

    e. Enter at 2 and exit at 5.

    f. Reenter at 5 and exit at 6.

    g. Enter at 7 and exit at 5.

    h. Enter again at 7 and exit at 5.

    i. Enter at 6 and exit at 5. Lock the stitch.

2. Paint the eyes using acrylic paint and a small paint brush. Paint the entire eye sockets with white paint. Let the paint dry. Paint blue eyeballs in the center of the white sockets.

Making Nell's eyes

1. To form Nell's eyes follow the entry and exit points given in Figure E.

    a. Enter at 1 and exit at 2.

    b. Reenter at 2 and exit at 6.

    c. Pull the thread across the surface, enter at 2 and exit at 3.

    d. Reenter at 3 and exit at 7.

    e. Pull the thread across the surface, enter at 3 and exit at 2. Gently pull the thread until the closed eyes appear. Lock the stitch.

    f. Reenter at 2 and exit at 1.

2. Lock the stitch and cut the thread.

Attaching the head

1. Gather the hose ¼ inch from the edge around the neckline opening using heavy-duty thread. Pull the gathering threads until the opening measures approximately 2 inches across.

2. Center the head over the opening. Carefully whipstitch completely around the neck several times to secure the head to the body.

Figure F

Figure G

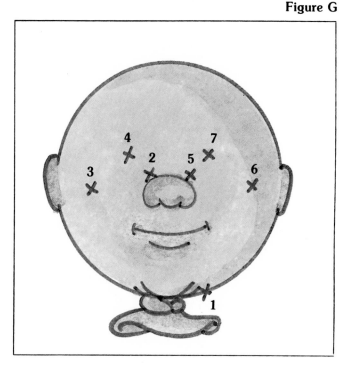

Figure K

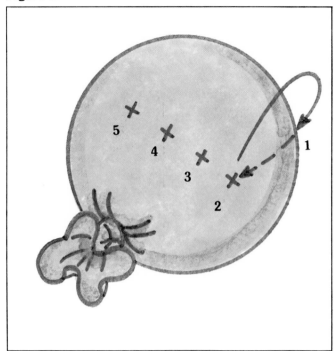

Figure H

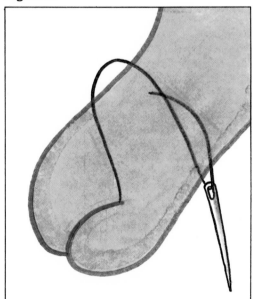

Figure I

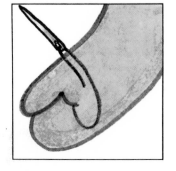

Figure J

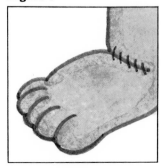

Feet

1. Insert the needle ½ inch from the seam line on the top of the foot. This will be the base of the first toe.

2. Wrap the thread around the end of the foot. Enter the needle on the bottom of the foot and exit on top of the foot where you began **(Figure H)**.

3. Pull the thread tightly to form 1 toe. Lock the stitch.

4. Enter at the point where you just exited. Take a ½ inch stitch under the surface and exit at the base of the second toe **(Figure I)**.

5. Repeat steps 2 through 4 three more times to form the remaining toes.

6. Bend the foot into an L-shaped ankle. Whipstitch the top of the foot to the front of the ankle and pull the thread tightly. Lock the stitch and cut the thread. **(Figure J)**.

Hands

1. Use the same technique to form the hands that you used to shape the toes. The first stitch will form the thumb, and should begin closer to the wrist than the other fingers.

2. Form a total of 5 fingers **(Figure K)**. Lock the last stitch.

3. Reenter where you exited and push the needle through the hand and exit on top of the wrist.

4. Wrap the thread around the outside of the wrist. Lock the stitch and cut the thread.

Figure L

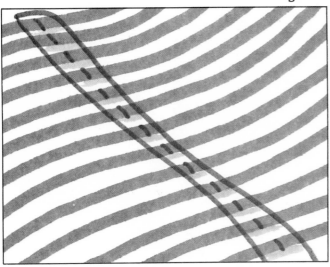

Making Nell's hair

1. Measure Nell's head from the center of the forehead to 2 inches below the center back of the head. Cut a length of seam binding to this measurement.

2. Cut the fiber into 20-inch lengths. Center the fiber lengths across the cut seam binding. Machine stitch down the center, spacing the fiber evenly along the stitching line **(Figure L)**. Make sure the binding is completely covered by the fiber.

3. Place the seam binding on the head to form a center part. Hand sew along the machine stitching to secure the fiber hair to the head.

4. Trim small bangs across the front of Nell's forehead. Divide the remaining fiber into halves along the part and braid each side. Tie thread around the ends of the braids. Cover the thread by tying ribbon bows on each braid. Glue or hand stitch the hair to the head around the hairline to hold it in place.

Making Ned's hair

1. Use heavy-duty thread to hand tack the free end of a yarn skein at the top of the forehead.

2. To make 1 curl, wrap the yarn around a pencil 20 times. Transfer the yarn loop from the pencil to a threaded needle. Stitch the yarn curl to the head **(Figure M)**.

3. Repeat step 2 until the head is completely covered with curls. When the thread becomes too short, lock the stitch into the head and rethread the needle.

4. When the last curl is secured, lock the stitch. Cut the yarn and tuck the end underneath a curl.

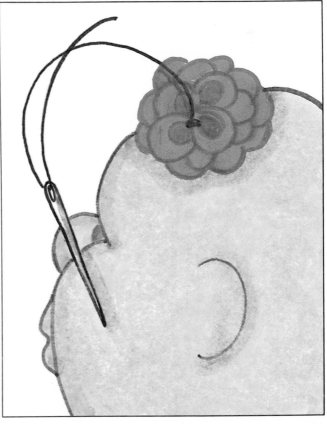

Figure N

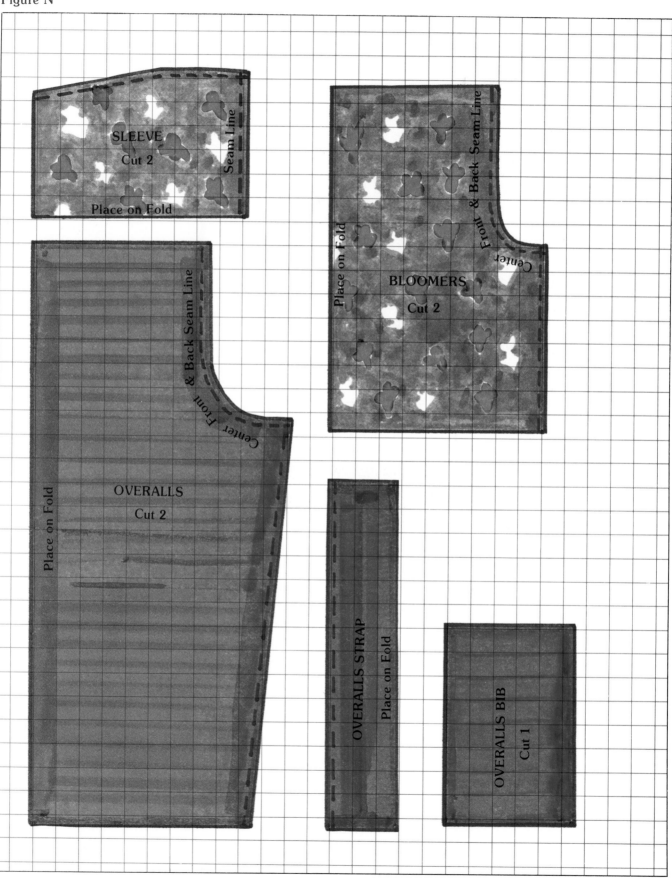

SLEEVE
Cut 2

Seam Line

Place on Fold

BLOOMERS
Cut 2

Place on Fold

Front & Back Seam Line

Center

OVERALLS
Cut 2

Place on Fold

Center Front & Back Seam Line

OVERALLS STRAP

Place on Fold

OVERALLS BIB

Cut 1

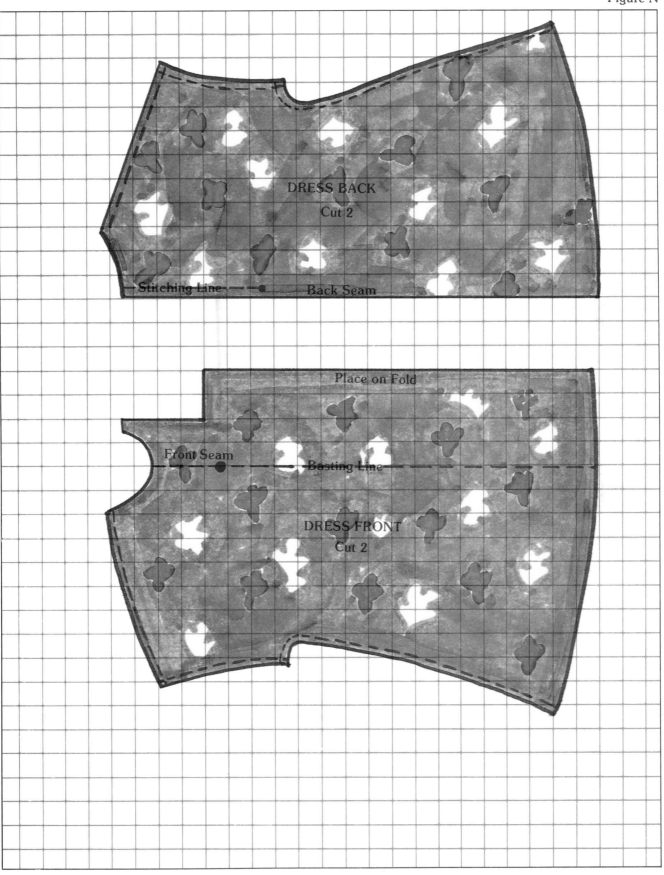

DRESS BACK
Cut 2

Stitching Line — • Back Seam

Place on Fold

Front Seam • Basting Line

DRESS FRONT
Cut 2

Figure O

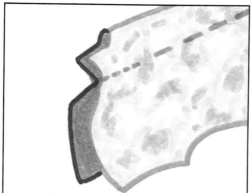

Figure P

Figure Q

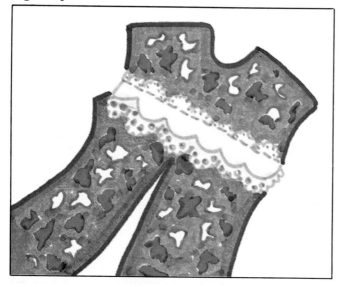

Figure R

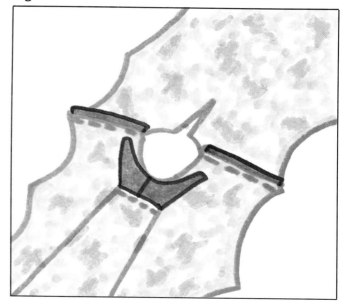

Making Nell's dress

1. Enlarge the clothing patterns given in **Figure N** to full size. Since each doll will vary somewhat in size depending upon the amount of stuffing, compare the enlarged pattern to the size of doll and adjust it if necessary before cutting the fabric. Use a ⅝-inch seam allowance on all seams.

2. Cut the specified number of each pattern piece from the appropriate color of fabric. Pay particular attention to the "place on fold" notations given.

3. Fold the Dress Front right sides together and sew the center front seam from the neckline to the small circle (**Figure O**). Baste the remainder of the seam from the small circle to the bottom edge.

4. Unfold the Dress Front on the wrong side, and press the basted pleat, dividing it equally on either side of the center seam. Stitch across the top of the pressed pleat (**Figure P**).

5. Remove the basting stitches and turn the dress to the right side. Sew 2-inch-wide flat lace across the dress front between the 2 armholes (**Figure Q**).

6. Place the 2 Dress Backs right sides together and stitch the center back seam from the bottom edge to the small circle. Leave the top 6 inches open and unstitched. Press the seam open.

7. Stitch the dress front to the dress back at the shoulder seams (**Figure R**). Press the seams open.

8. Sew the sleeves to the dress, placing right sides together.

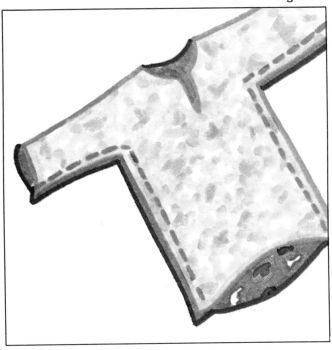

Figure S

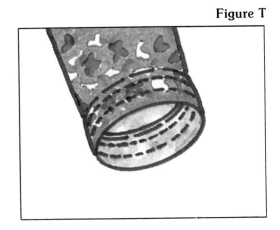

Figure T

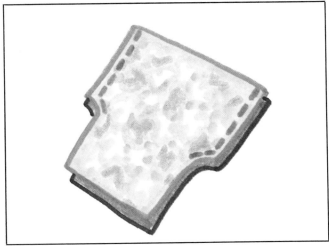

Figure U

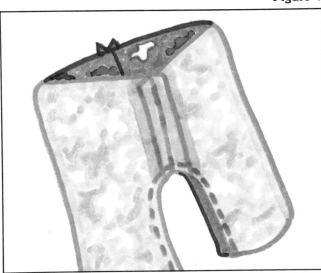

Figure V

9. Turn the dress wrong side out and stitch the underarm and side seams (**Figure S**).

10. To make casings for elastic in the sleeves, press the raw edges to the wrong side. Turn under a 1-inch hem and stitch. Stitch the hem again ⅜ inch from the hem stitching to form the casing (**Figure T**). Leave a small opening in the stitching to insert the elastic.

11. Topstitch eyelet trim around the bottom of each sleeve.

12. Cut a 6-inch length of elastic and insert it through the sleeve casing. Stitch the ends of the elastic securely together.

13. Pull the elastic into the casing and whipstitch the opening together.

14. Encase the dress neckline in seam binding. Sew a hook and eye closure to the neck opening.

15. Hem the bottom edge of the dress to the desired length. Topstitch eyelet trim to the bottom of the dress.

Making Nell's bloomers

1. Pin the 2 Bloomers right sides together, and stitch the center front and back seams (**Figure U**).

2. Match the center front seam and the center back seam and stitch the inner leg seam (**Figure V**).

3. Make elastic casings at waist and leg openings of the bloomers in the same manner as you did for the dress sleeves, fitting the bloomers to the doll.

Figure X

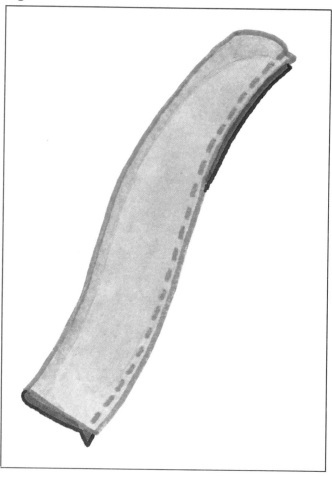

Making Ned's overalls

1. Make Ned's overalls using the same procedure used for Nell's bloomers (steps 1 and 2).

2. Hem all 4 edges of the Bib and sew one long side of the hemmed bib to the overalls at the top center front **(Figure W).**

3. Fold the Strap lengthwise with right sides together and stitch **(Figure X).** Turn the sewn straps right side out and press. Repeat for remaining Strap piece.

4. Hand tack the straps to the back of the overalls at the waistline. Pull the overalls onto the doll and adjust the straps to fit the shoulders. Hand tack the free end of the straps underneath the bib top. Sew buttons on the bib top over the straps.

5. Fold the excess fabric on both sides of the overalls to form a pleat. Hand tack the pleat in place, fitting the overalls snugly to the body. Sew buttons on top of each pleat.

6. Hem the bottom of each overall leg to fit the doll.

Circus Crib Mobile

The bright colors of the circus animals and ringmaster clown will provide lots of visual stimulation for your baby as they bounce and turn in the breeze.

Figure A

Materials

1 pair of nurse's white pantyhose.
1 leg of navy blue knee-high hose.
1 pair of gray-colored "winter" pantyhose.
8-inch diameter metal ring.
1 yard of brightly striped fabric.
1½ yards of ½-inch-wide pre-gathered eyelet trim.
2-inch-diameter gold metal ring.
4-inch length of 1-inch-wide green satin ribbon.
1 yard of red rick-rack.
½ pound of polyester fiberfill.
Small amount of yellow fiber.
Four ½-inch-diameter gold metal rings.
Scraps of orange yarn.
Scraps of blue, white, and red felt.
½ yard of narrow gold braid.
2 pompoms: 1 red and 1 black.
Red and black felt-tip markers.
Heavy-duty thread and a long sharp needle.
6 small black beads.
Scissors, glue, and yellow spray paint.
Tracing paper and a pencil.

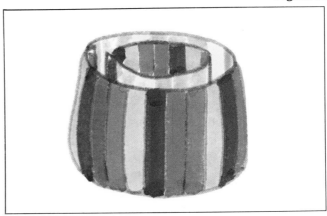

Making the canopy

1.   Cut a 24 x 28-inch rectangle from the striped fabric, and fold it in half lengthwise. Stitch a ¼-inch seam along the long edge. Fold the resulting tube in half, turning it back over itself so the seam is on the inside and the raw edges are together **(Figure A)**.

55

Figure B

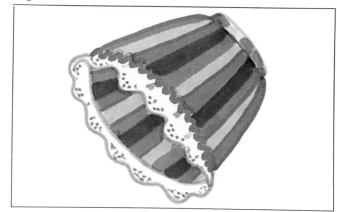

2. Stitch the pregathered eyelet trim over the folded edge of the tube **(Figure B)**. Stitch red rick-rack over the top edge of the eyelet trim.

3. Slip an 8-inch-diameter metal ring between the 2 layers of the canopy through the raw edges at the top.

4. Fold the raw edges along the top to the inside and topstitch in place.

5. Sew long gathering stitches around the stitched top, 2 inches from the edge. Pull the gathering threads tightly to gather the top together **(Figure C)**.

6. Wrap a 4-inch length of green satin ribbon around the gathers and whipstitch it in place, turning the raw edges under.

7. Sew a 2-inch-diameter gold ring to the gathered top of the canopy.

Figure C

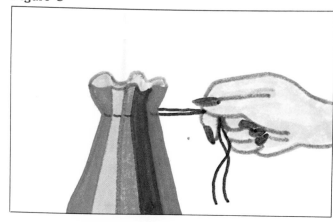

Figure D

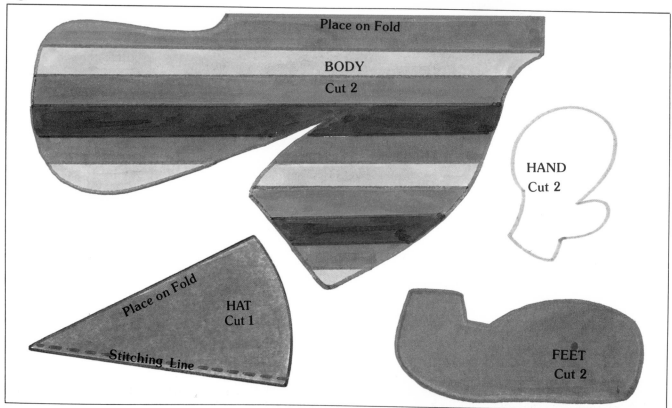

Place on Fold

BODY
Cut 2

HAND
Cut 2

Place on Fold

HAT
Cut 1

Stitching Line

FEET
Cut 2

56

Figure E

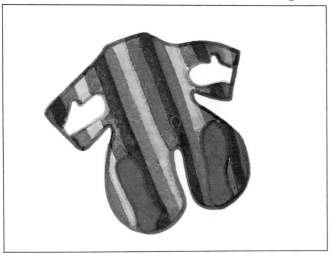

Figure F

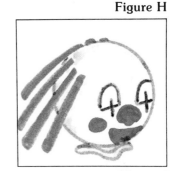

Figure G

Figure H

Figure I

Figure J

Making the clown

1. Full-size patterns for the clown are given in **Figure D.** Trace the patterns with tracing paper and pencil. Cut the following pieces: 2 Body pieces from striped fabric, 2 Hand pieces from white felt, 2 Foot pieces from red felt, and 1 Hat piece from blue felt.

2. Place the 2 Hand and 2 Foot pieces on the right side of 1 Body piece, as shown in **Figure E.**

3. Pin the 2 Body pieces right sides together. Stitch a ¼-inch seam around the body, being careful to keep the feet and hands out of the seam allowance. Leave the neck open and unstitched **(Figure F).**

4. Cut a 1-inch slit in the back neckline. Turn the body right side out and press.

5. Stuff the body lightly with polyester fiberfill and whipstitch the slit in the neck closed.

6. Form a small 1-inch-diameter of polyester fiberfill for the clown's head. Cut a 2-inch-diameter circle of white hose and wrap it around the fiberfill ball. Tie the raw edges of the hose together with thread on the bottom of the head.

7. Paint a clown face on the hose-covered head as illustrated in **Figure G** using black and red felt-tip markers.

8. Whipstitch the completed head to the body, inserting the tied hose area inside the neck opening.

9. Whipstitch eyelet trim around the neck.

10. Glue short strands of orange yarn to the head **(Figure H).**

11. Fold the Hat in half and stitch ¼-inch from the edge as shown in **Figure I.** Turn the hat right side out, and whipstitch it securely to the top of the head over the top of the yarn hair.

12. Stitch a red pompom to the top of the hat.

13. Fold the top of the hat down, and whipstitch a small gold ring to the fold **(Figure J).**

Making the lion

1. Trim the toe section from a leg of white pantyhose, 6 inches above the toe seam.

2. Stuff the hose, and tie it off-center at the bottom (**Figure K**). The knot will later be covered by the tail.

3. Tie a string around the middle to separate the head from the body.

Forming the facial features

1. To form the features, follow the entry and exit points illustrated in **Figure L**. Use heavy-duty thread and a long sharp needle.

    a. Enter at 1 and exit at 2.

    b. Sew a large clockwise circle of basting stitches, ending at 3. Pull the thread and lock the stitch.

    c. Enter at 2 and exit at 4.

    d. Enter at 3 and exit at 2.

    e. Enter at 4 and exit at 5. Pull the thread and lock the stitch.

    f. Enter at 4 and exit at 6.

    g. Enter at 7 and exit at 2. Pull the thread and lock the stitch.

    h. Reenter at 2 and exit at 1. Lock the stitch and cut the thread.

2. To form the arms, pinch up a ridge across the chest. Stitch back and forth under the ridge, returning to the top center of the ridge.

3. Take a vertical stitch across the arm ridge and return to the center top. Tighten the thread to separate the arms and lock the stitch (**Figure M**).

4. Repeat steps 4 and 5 at the bottom of the lion's body to form the legs.

Making the tail

1. Cut a 1 x 4-inch rectangle of white pantyhose. Fold the rectangle lengthwise, and sew a ¼-inch seam along the side and across 1 end (**Figure N**).

2. Turn the stitched tube right side out, and stuff it with polyester fiberfill.

3. Turn the raw edges around the opening to the inside. Fit the open end of the tail over the knot at the back of the lion's body and whipstitch it in place (**Figure O**).

Figure K

Figure L

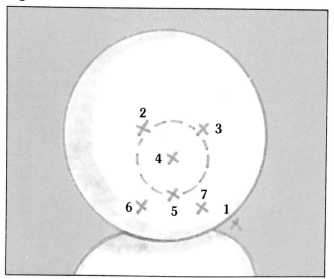

Figure M

Figure N

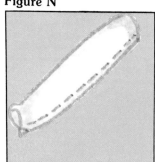

Figure P

Figure Q

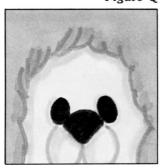

Figure R

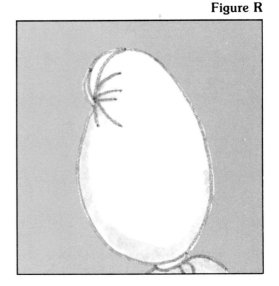

Figure S

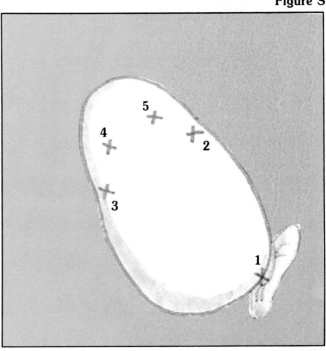

Finishing the lion

1.   Spray the completed body with yellow paint and allow it to dry overnight.

2.   Glue a small amount of yellow fiber to the top of the head and around the face for the mane, and to the tip of the tail **(Figure P).**

3.   Bend the tail around to the front of the body and tack it in place.

4.   Wrap gold braid around the lion's neck and whipstitch it together in the back.

5.   Glue black beads in the eye indentations.

6.   Color the nose with a black marker **(Figure Q).**

Making the seal

1.   Tie a knot in the toe of a white pantyhose. Cut 8 inches above the knot. Turn the hose so the knot is on the inside.

2.   Stuff the hose with polyester fiberfill, leaving the last 2 inches unstuffed. Tie off the stuffing with heavy-duty thread, leaving the excess hose intact.

3.   Manipulate the knot at the bottom to the side, as shown in **Figure R.**

4.   Follow the entry and exit points illustrated in **Figure S** to shape the seal's features.

   a.   Enter at 1 and exit at 2.

   b.   Pull the thread over the surface. Enter at 3 and exit at 4.

   c.   Pull the thread tightly to form the neck, and lock the stitch.

   d.   Reenter at 4 and exit at 5.

   e.   Reenter at 5 and exit at 4. Pull the thread to form the eye indentations and lock the stitch.

   f.   Reenter at 4 and exit at 1. Lock the stitch and cut the thread.

5.   To form the flippers, pinch up a vertical ridge across the chest. Stitch back and forth under the ridge, returning to the top of the center of the ridge.

Figure V

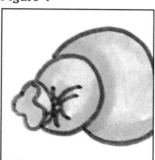

Figure W

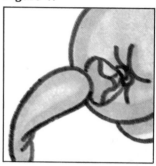

6. Take a vertical stitch down the center of the ridge and return to the top. Pull the thread to separate the flippers and lock the stitch **(Figure T).**

7. To form the tail, stuff the excess hose below the knot lightly with polyester fiberfill. Turn the raw edges to the inside and whipstitch them together, pulling the thread at the end to draw the ends of the tailfin together **(Figure U).**

Finishing the seal

1. Form a 2-inch-diameter ball of polyester fiberfill, and cover it with a 4-inch-diameter circle cut from opaque blue "winter" hose. Tie the raw edges of the hose together at the bottom with heavy-duty thread.

2. Cut off the excess hose around the gathers. Whipstitch the completed ball to the seal, positioning the gathered area just below the 2 front flippers.

3. Glue black beads in the eye indentations. Glue a black pompom on the end of the nose.

4. Whipstitch a small gold metal ring to the center of the seal's back.

Making the elephant

1. Tie a knot in a leg of opaque gray-colored "winter" hose at the panty line. Cut just above the knot. Cut again 8 inches below the knot. Turn the hose so the knot is on the inside.

2. Stuff 4 inches of the hose to form the body and tie the hose in a knot.

3. Continue stuffing to form a slightly smaller ball for the head. Tie the hose again, centering the knot as shown in **Figure V.** Trim off the excess hose.

4. To make the trunk, cut a 1 x 3-inch rectangle of gray hose.

5. Fold the hose rectangle lengthwise and sew a ¼-inch seam down the long side and across 1 end to form a tube.

Figure T

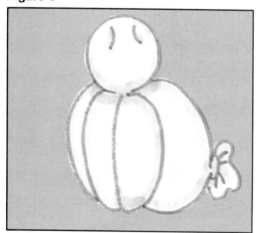

Figure U

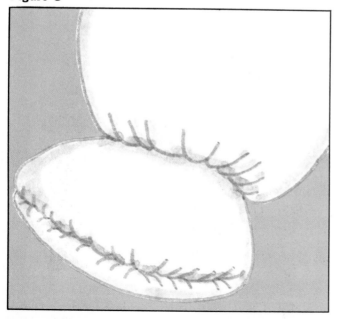

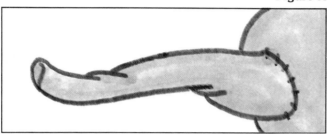

Figure X

6. Turn the tube right side out and stuff it with polyester fiberfill.

7. Turn the raw edges around the opening to the inside and whipstitch the tube to the head, placing the trunk opening over the knot in the head (**Figure W**).

8. Bend the trunk into shape as shown in **Figure X**.

9. Glue black beads on the head for eyes.

Figure Y

Finishing the elephant

1. To make the elephant's ears, cut 2 rectangles from gray hose, each measuring 2 x 4 inches.

2. Place the 2 rectangles together and stitch a ¼-inch seam around the edges, leaving a small opening in the center of 1 edge (**Figure Y**).

3. Turn the stitched rectangle right side out and whipstitch the opening closed.

4. Whipstitch the ears to the back of the head.

5. Stitch the head to the body where the ears are joined (**Figure Z**).

Figure Z

6. Cut a small triangle of hose and glue it to the end of the body to form the tail.

7. Cut 4 rectangles for the legs from gray hose, each measuring 2 x 4 inches. Fold the rectangles in half and stitch the side and end to form a tube.

8. Turn the tubes right side out. Stuff each tube with polyester fiberfill.

9. Turn the raw edges on the open end to the inside. Whipstitch all 4 legs to the lower portion of the body (**Figure AA**).

Figure AA

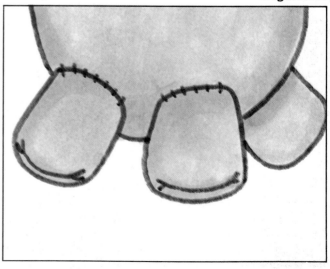

10. To make the blanket for the elephant, cut a 1 x 5-inch rectangle of red felt. Glue a 5-inch length of gold braid down the center of the rectangle.

11. Cut off all 4 corners of the red felt blanket and whipstitch it across the elephant's back.

12. Sew a small gold ring to the center back.

Final assembly

1. Suspend the canopy with heavy-duty thread tied around the top ring.

2. Tie thread through the small rings on each of the animals and the clown, and suspend them by sewing the thread around the lower edge of the canopy.

Animal Slippers

These easy-to-make slippers will keep a child's feet warm and comfortable on even the coldest winter days.

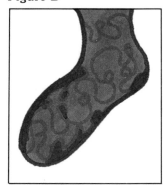

Materials

1 pair of blue heavy "winter" pantyhose.
12-inch square of buckram or other stiffener.
½-inch length of brightly striped ribbon.
¼ yard of heavy yellow felt.
4 red buttons.
Heavy-duty blue sewing thread.
Polyester fiberfill.
Sewing needle, sewing thread, scissors, straight pins.
Heavy cardboard, newspapers, paper, and pencil.

Making the sole

1. To make the pattern for the slippers, have the child stand on a piece of paper, and trace around his foot with a pencil. Use the paper pattern to cut 8 sole pieces: 4 pieces from yellow felt, 2 from heavy cardboard, and 2 from buckram.

2. Place 2 felt soles together, sandwiching a buckram sole between the layers of felt. Topstitch the 3 layers together ¼ inch from the edge to make 1 slipper sole **(Figure A)**.

3. Repeat step 2 to make the sole for the other slipper.

Figure A	Figure B
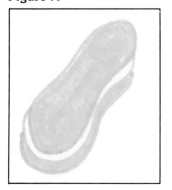	

Making the slipper

1. Cut off 1 leg of blue "winter" hose at the panty line.

2. Temporarily insert 1 cardboard shoe sole inside the toe of the hose leg so that you can determine the size of the slipper.

3. Stuff the inside of the hose above the sole with newspapers to form a "foot" over which to make the slipper **(Figure B)**.

Figure C

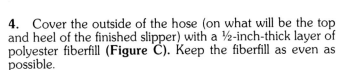

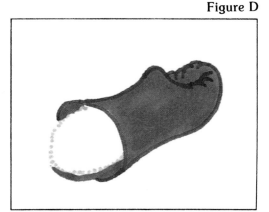

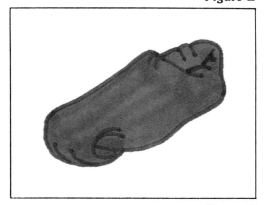

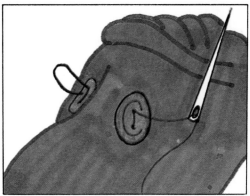

4. Cover the outside of the hose (on what will be the top and heel of the finished slipper) with a ½-inch-thick layer of polyester fiberfill **(Figure C)**. Keep the fiberfill as even as possible.

5. Pull the remaining hose back over the polyester fiberfill so that the opening in the hose is at the toe of the slipper **(Figure D)**.

6. Fold the open end of the hose to the bottom of the slipper and whipstitch it securely in place **(Figure E)**.

Sewing the face

1. Pinch up a ridge down the front of the slipper top. Sew a red button on each side of the ridge, as shown in **Figure F,** stitching back and forth under the ridge to connect the 2 buttons.

2. A full-size pattern for the ears is given in **Figure G.** Trace the pattern and cut 2 ears from yellow felt.

3. Whipstitch the ears over the red button eyes at the top of the slipper.

4. Tie a striped ribbon bow, and hand tack it over an ear.

Finishing

1. Pin 1 yellow felt sole to the bottom of the foot, adjusting the fiberfill inside the hose wherever necessary to fit.

2. Backstitch around the sole using heavy-duty blue thread, stitching completely through the hose and all sole layers **(Figure H)**.

3. Repeat the entire procedure to make the other slipper.

4. Remove the newspaper and cardboard forms.

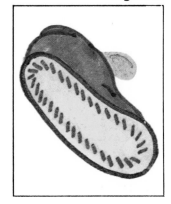

Ballerina Marionette

This fanciful figure will dance her way into your heart. She is an actual working model, and moves with realistic grace.

Materials

1 pair of nurse's white pantyhose.
1 pair of regular pantyhose.
½ pound of polyester fiberfill.
2 yards of nylon netting.
¼ yard of pink satin fabric.
½ yard of white cotton fabric.
Brown fiber.
12-inch length of threaded sequins.
½ yard of 1-inch-wide pregathered lace.
1 silver pipecleaner.
½ yard of narrow pink satin ribbon.
5-inch length of 2-inch-wide decorative trim.
3-foot length of ¾-inch-wide flat craft stick.
1 can of clear acrylic spray.
Glue, scissors, spring-type clothespins, pink and white sewing thread, needle, iron, and ironing board.
Heavy-duty white thread and a long sharp needle.
Paper and pencil to enlarge the patterns.

Making the legs

1. Enlarge the patterns given in **Figure A** to full size. Cut 4 Leg pieces from white cotton fabric.

2. Place 2 Leg pieces right sides together and stitch a ¼-inch seam around the edges, leaving the top open and unstitched. Clip the seams and turn the leg right side out.

3. Stuff the leg tightly and evenly to the knee. Tie the knee with heavy-duty white thread. Continue stuffing the rest of the leg to within ½ inch of the top opening **(Figure B)**.

4. Repeat steps 2 and 3 for the remaining 2 Leg pieces to form the other leg.

Making the body

1. Cut 2 Body pieces from pink satin fabric.

2. Place 1 Body piece right side up on a flat surface. Position the stuffed legs (heels together) even with 1 narrow end of the Body, as illustrated in **Figure C**. Baste the legs in place.

Figure A

LEG Cut 4

BODY

Cut 2

SLIPPER

Cut 4

Figure B

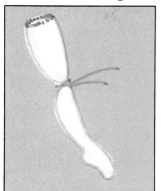

Figure C

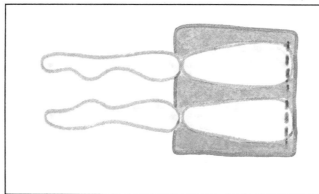

Figure D

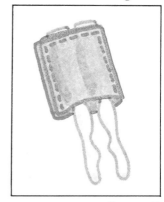

Figure E

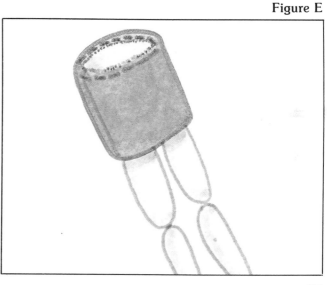

3. Place the remaining Body (right side down) on top of the legs, and pin it in place.

4. Stitch across the end and down both sides of the body **(Figure D).** Be careful to keep the legs out of the seam allowance.

5. Fold the body up and stuff it lightly to within 1 inch of the top. Turn the top edge under ¼ inch **(Figure E).**

Making the chest and head

1. Tie a knot in a leg of pantyhose at the panty line. Cut 1 inch above the knot, and cut off the toe seam. Turn the hose so the knot is on the inside.

2. Shape a 5-inch-diameter ball of polyester fiberfill, and insert it inside the hose to form the head. Tie a knot in the hose at the neck.

65

Figure F

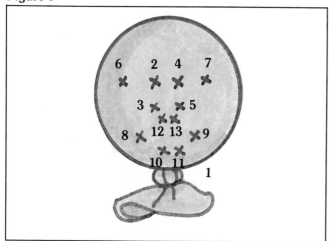

Figure G

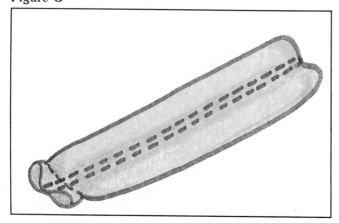

3. To form the facial features, follow the entry and exit points illustrated in **Figure F.**

    a.   Enter at 1 and exit at 2.

    b.   Enter at 3 and exit at 4.

    c.   Enter at 5 and exit at 2. Pull the thread to tighten and lock the stitch.

    d.   Reenter at 2 and exit at 3.

    e.   Enter at 5 and exit at 4. Pull the thread and lock the stitch.

    f.   Reenter at 4 and exit at 12.

    g.   Reenter at 12 and exit at 2.

    h.   Reenter at 2 and exit at 13.

    i.   Reenter at 13 and exit at 4. Pull the thread and lock the stitch.

    j.   Reenter at 4 and exit at 6.

    k.   Enter at 2 and exit at 7.

    l.   Enter at 4 and exit at 2. Pull the thread and lock the stitch.

    m.   Reenter at 2 and exit at 8.

    n.   Enter at 9 and exit at 4. Pull the thread and lock the stitch.

    o.   Reenter at 4 and exit at 10.

    p.   Enter at 11 and exit at 2. Pull the thread and lock the stitch.

4. Draw lips on the face using a red felt-tip marker. Draw eyelashes and eyebrows with a black felt-tip marker. Brush powdered cheek blusher on the ballerina's cheeks.

Making the arms

1. Cut the remaining leg of regular pantyhose at the panty line. Cut away the toe seam.

2. Sew 2 seams, ¼ inch apart, down the center of the hose, and across 1 end **(Figure G).** Stretch the hose gently as you stitch to retain the elasticity.

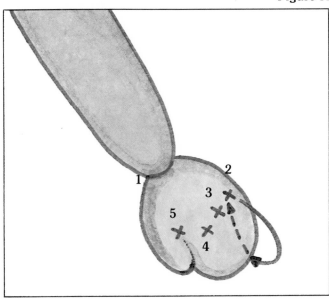

3. Cut carefully between the 2 sewn seams to form 2 arm pieces. Turn the 2 arms right side out.

4. Stuff the arms with polyester fiberfill until they are 12 inches long. Keep the 2 arms equal to each other in size.

5. Tie thread around the wrist of each arm, 2 inches from the closed end of the arm. Tie a knot in the open end of the hose.

6. To form the fingers on the hand, follow the entry and exit points illustrated in **Figure H.**

    a. Enter at 1 and exit at 2.

    b. Wrap the thread around the end of the hand to the other side. Enter behind 2 and exit at 2.

    c. Pull the thread and lock the stitch to form the first finger.

    d. Reenter at 2 and exit at 3.

    e. Wrap the thread around the end of the hand to the other side. Enter behind 3 and exit at 3.

    f. Pull the thread and lock the stitch. Reenter at 3 and exit at 4.

    g. Wrap the thread around the end of the hand to the other side. Enter behind 4 and exit at 4.

    h. Pull the thread and lock the stitch. Reenter at 4 and exit at 5.

    i. Pinch up a ridge on the side of the hand to form the thumb. Wrap the thread around the end of the ridge. Enter behind 5 and exit at 5.

    j. Pull the thread to form the thumb and lock the stitch.

7. Repeat step 6 on the remaining arm to form the other hand.

8. Place the 2 completed arms and the head/chest on newspapers, and spray with clear acrylic spray paint. After they have dried, turn them over and spray the other sides. Again, let them dry.

Figure I

Figure J

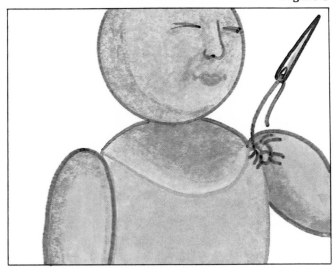

Assembling the body

1. Insert the chest in the top of the body. Whipstitch around the neckline several times to secure the body to the chest **(Figure I).**

2. Trim excess hose from the knot in the arms. Stitch the arms to the sides of the doll at the neckline **(Figure J).** Stitch only through the knot to allow the arms to move freely.

Figure K

Figure L

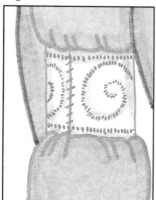

Figure M

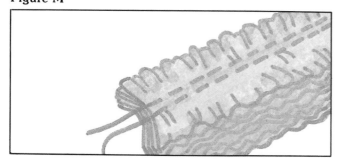

Figure N

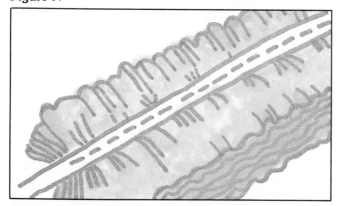

Figure O

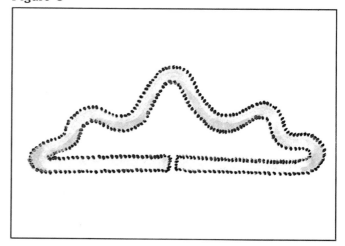

Clothing and trim

1. Whipstitch ½-inch-wide pre-gathered lace around the neckline, beginning and ending at the center back. Whipstitch sequins over the top edge of the lace (**Figure K).**

2. Wrap a 5-inch length of 2-inch-wide trim around the center of the body to form the waistline, and whipstitch it together in the back of the body (**Figure L).**

3. To make the tutu, cut the net into 8 rectangles, each measuring 8 x 24 inches. Stack the rectangles on top of each other, and sew gathering stitches down the center of the stack (**Figure M).**

4. Pull the gathering threads until the gathers measure the same size as the ballerina's hips.

5. Center an 18-inch length of ribbon over the gathers and stitch it to the net (**Figure N).**

6. Fold the gathered net together over the ribbon and wrap the tutu around the ballerina's hips. Tie the ribbon in a bow at the center back. Separate the layers of net to form the tutu.

7. Coil the brown fiber around the head. Begin at the back hairline, and continue wrapping around the head to form a high bun at the top. Glue the fiber in place around the hairline and during the wrapping to secure it in place.

8. Bend a silver pipecleaner into a tiara as shown in **Figure O.**

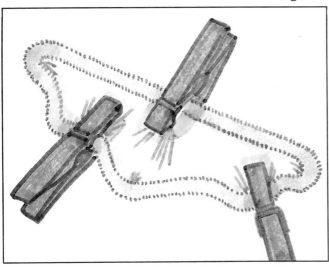

9. Wipe glue on 1 side of the pipecleaner and stretch a piece of white pantyhose over the glue. Hold the stretched hose in place with clothespins until the glue dries **(Figure P).** Cut around the outside of the pipecleaner with scissors to eliminate the excess hose.

10. Bend the completed tiara into a semi-circle and glue it to the top of the ballerina's head.

Making the tights

1. Cut 1 leg of white pantyhose at the panty line. Sew 2 seams, ½ inch apart, down the center of the hose **(Figure Q).** Stretch the hose gently as you sew.

2. Cut carefully between the 2 sewn seams to form the 2 tights. Turn the tights right side out.

3. Slip the tights over the legs, positioning the seams at the back. Roll the tights up at the top of the legs.

Making the slippers

1. Cut 4 Slipper pieces from pink satin fabric using the full-size pattern.

2. Place 2 Slipper pieces right sides together, and sew a ¼-inch seam, leaving the opening for the foot unstitched **(Figure R).**

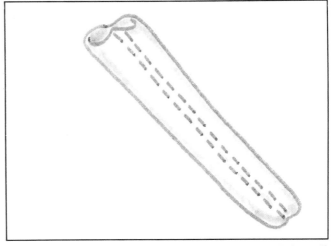

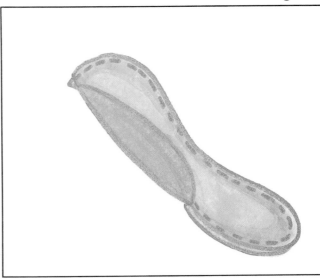

Figure S

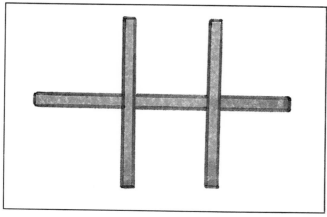

Figure T

3. Turn the slipper right side out. Turn the raw edges on the foot opening to the inside and press.

4. Repeat steps 2 and 3 for the remaining Slipper pieces.

5. Fit the slippers over the ballerina's feet and whipstitch around the foot opening to secure them.

6. Wrap a narrow pink ribbon around each of the ankles and tie it in a bow in the front.

Making the manipulator

1. Cut the wood craft sticks into 4 pieces: 3 pieces each 8 inches long, and 1 piece 12 inches long.

2. Arrange 3 of the pieces and glue them together as shown in **Figure S.** Clamp the glued joints with clothespins until they dry. The remaining piece is used to control the legs. It is not permanently attached to the manipulator. It can be held separately in the left hand, or balanced behind the front crosspiece on top of the manipulator.

3. Cut seven 3-foot lengths of heavy-duty white thread. Stitch 1 of the lengths to each hand, each knee, the top of the head, and to the chest at the back of each arm.

4. Tie the free ends of the strings around the crosspieces on the manipulator as illustrated in **Figure T.**

5. Adjust the strings to the proper length. Glue each string to the crosspiece to make sure it stays in place.

THE PERFECT TOUCH

... for your home decor

The Gork

This household elf is a valuable asset to any home. If you can lure him to take up residence in your home, the fires will always burn brightly, the cupboards will always be well stocked, and cheerfulness will abound.

Materials

½ yard of 36-inch-wide green pre-quilted calico fabric.
¼ yard of 36-inch-wide yellow felt.
½ yard of white cotton fabric.
1 pantyhose leg.
1 pound of bonded polyester fiberfill.
½ yard of narrow green grosgrain ribbon.
4-inch square of cardboard.
¼-inch-diameter wooden dowel rod, 11 inches long.
Paper and pencil to enlarge the patterns.
Green embroidery thread and needle.
A small amount of your favorite sachet to fill the Gork's special
    bag (or make a sweet-smelling mixture using a teaspoon
    each of cinnamon, cloves, thyme, and marjoram).
String, straight pins, sewing thread to match the fabrics, iron,
    ironing board, and nylon sewing thread.

Making the body

1. Cut the foot from a pantyhose about 2 inches above the ankle.

2. Form a small ball of fiberfill about 19 inches in circumference. Compress and stuff the batting inside the pantyhose foot until you have formed a round "head" about 13 inches in circumference **(Figure A)**.

3. To make the body, form a larger ball of fiberfill beneath the head. When compressed, the body should be 16 inches in circumference, and 7 inches tall.

4. Tie a piece of string around the "neck." To prevent the head from wobbling, tie the string around a generous amount of fiberfill.

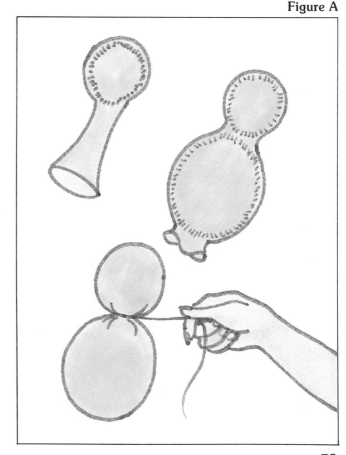

Figure B

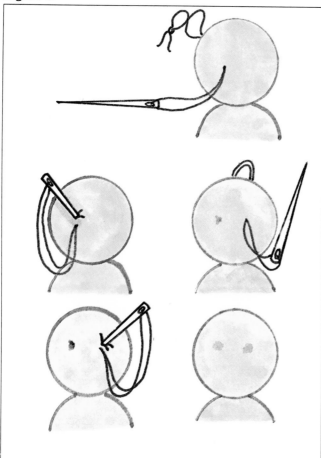

5. Thread a needle with nylon thread and follow the illustrations given in **Figure B** to form the eyes. Insert the threaded needle at the back of the head and bring it out on the left side of the face area. Take a small stitch and push the needle to the back of the head again. Pull the thread to form an eye dimple. Repeat on the other side of the face.

7. Embroider the eye sockets with a full strand of green embroidery thread using the satin stitch. Illustrated embroidery stitch instructions are given in the "Tips and Techniques" section at the beginning of this book.

8. Follow the illustrations given in **Figure C** to form the nose. Shape a small piece of fiberfill into a cone about 3 inches long and 2 inches in diameter at the widest point.

9. Wrap a small piece of hose over the fiberfill cone and sew the hose pieces together on what will be the underside of the nose. When sewn, the nose should measure 1 inch across the bottom and about 2 inches in length.

10. Sew the nose to the center of the face between the 2 eyes.

Figure C

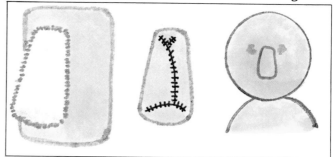

Figure D

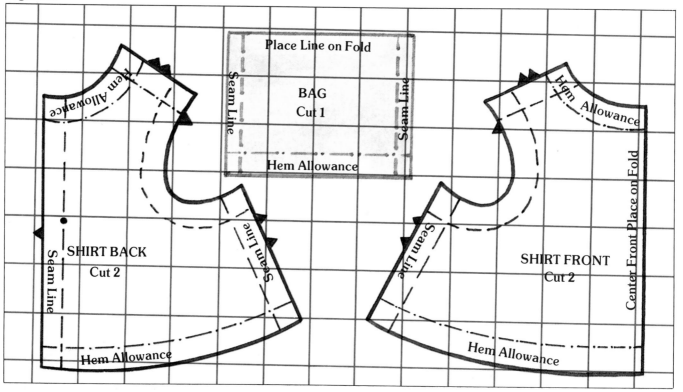

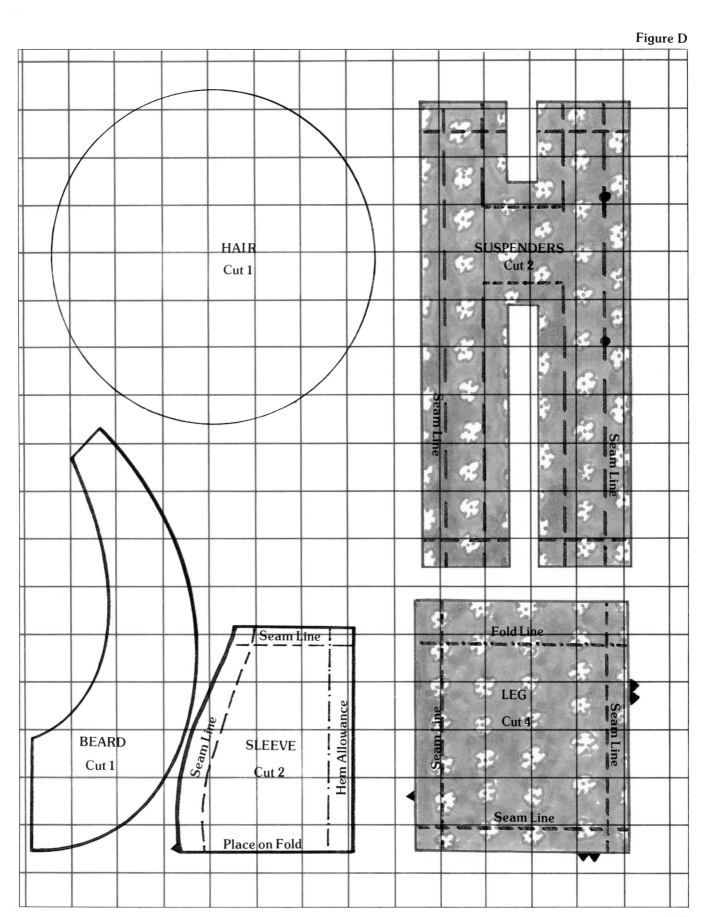

HAIR
Cut 1

SUSPENDERS
Cut 2

Seam Line

Seam Line

BEARD
Cut 1

Seam Line

SLEEVE
Cut 2

Seam Line

Hem Allowance

Place on Fold

Fold Line

LEG
Cut 4

Seam Line

Seam Line

Seam Line

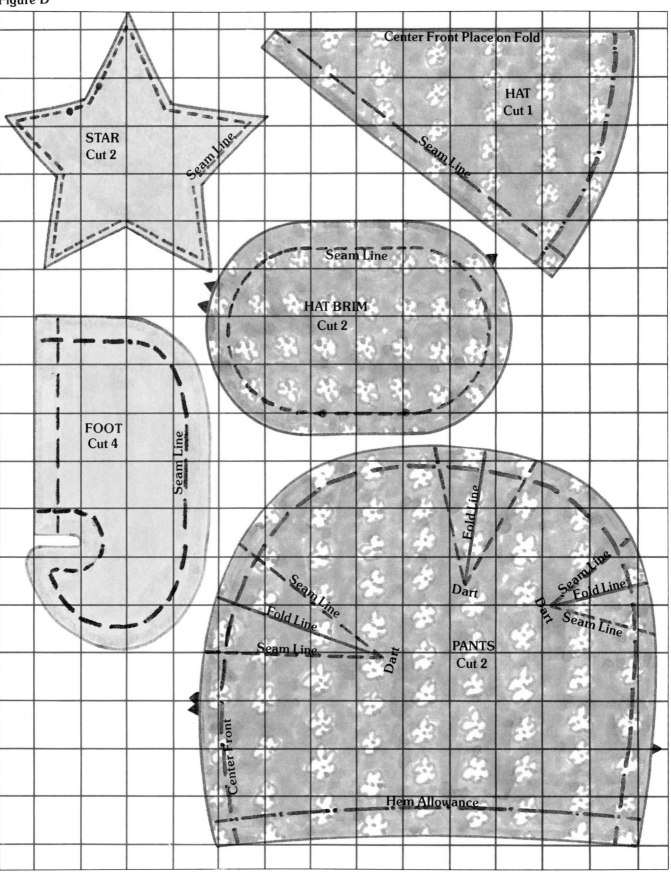

STAR
Cut 2

Center Front Place on Fold

HAT
Cut 1

Seam Line

Seam Line

HAT BRIM
Cut 2

Seam Line

FOOT
Cut 4

Seam Line

Fold Line

Dart

Seam Line

Seam Line

Fold Line

Dart

Seam Line

Fold Line

Seam Line

PANTS
Cut 2

Dart

Center Front

Hem Allowance

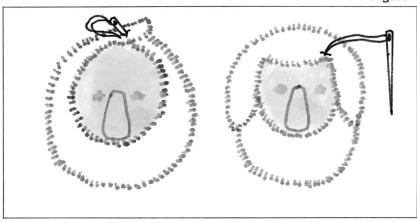

Figure E

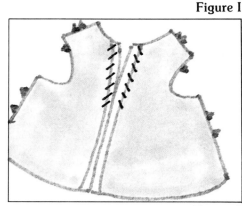

Figure F

Figure G

Figure H

Figure I

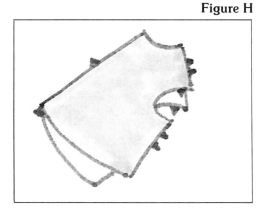

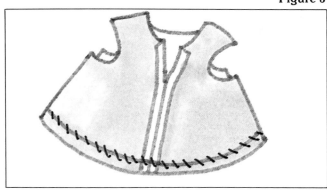

Figure J

Adding the beard

1. Enlarge the patterns given in **Figure D** to full size. Be sure to transfer notches and "place on fold" notations marked on each pattern piece.

2. Cut a beard from fiberfill using the full-size pattern. Wrap the beard around the bottom of the face and tack the ends at the top of the head **(Figure E)**.

3. Cut the hair from fiberfill using the full-size pattern. Tack it to the top of the head just above the eyes, and at the hairline on both sides of the face.

Making the arms

1. Cut a 10-inch length of hose for the arms. Form a 12-inch-long cylinder of fiberfill 2 inches in diameter. Pull the 10-inch hose over the 12-inch cylinder. Pull the ends of the hose until they extend about 2 inches past the ends of the cylinder. Fold the hose ends back over themselves, and tie a piece of string around the "wrist" to hold them in place **(Figure F)**.

2. Tie a piece of string in the middle of the arms. Hand tack the arms to the back of the neck **(Figure G)**.

Making the clothes

1. Cut the following pieces from white cotton fabric: 1 Shirt Front, 2 Shirt Backs, 2 Shirt Sleeves, and 1 Bag. Pay particular attention to the "place on fold" notations on the pattern pieces.

2. Place the 2 Shirt Backs right sides together. Sew the center back seam from the bottom to the small circle as shown in **Figure H**. Press the seam open.

3. Fold over the seam allowance on the remaining unstitched portion of the center back seam. Hem the edges and press them as shown in **Figure I**.

4. With right sides together, sew the Shirt Front to the Shirt Back along the shoulder seams **(Figure J)**.

5. Turn up the hem allowance on the shirt bottom and stitch.

Figure K

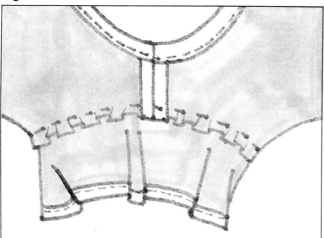

Figure L

Figure M

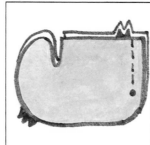

Figure N

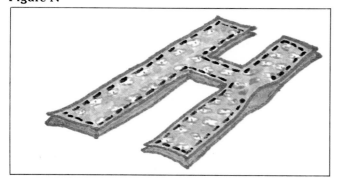

6. Press the shoulder seam flat. Hem the neck opening and press **(Figure K).**

7. Hem the bottom of the sleeve. Pin the sleeve to the armhole, right sides together, easing to fit. Stitch.

8. Sew the shirt back to the shirt front along the side and underarm seams.

9. Slip the finished shirt over the Gork's head. Hand tack the shirt together at the back of the neck opening.

Figure O

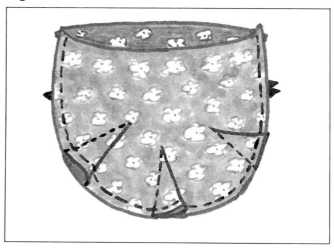

Wand and feet

1. Cut 2 Stars and 4 Foot pieces from yellow felt. Cut 1 Star piece from heavy cardboard.

2. Pin the 2 yellow felt Star pieces wrong sides together. Sandwich the cardboard Star piece between the 2 layers of felt to add stability.

3. Topstitch along the stitching lines, leaving an opening between the small circles as shown in **Figure L.**

4. Insert the wood dowel inside the stitched star. Hand tack through all thicknesses to hold the dowel in place.

5. Tie a ribbon bow around the dowel below the star.

6. Sew 2 Foot pieces together, sewing the seam to the small circles as shown in **Figure M.** Repeat for the remaining 2 Foot pieces. Set the assembled pieces aside.

Suspenders, pants and legs

1. Cut the following pieces from green calico fabric: 1 Hat, 2 Pants, 4 Legs, 2 Suspenders and 2 Hat Brims.

2. Place 2 Suspender pieces right sides together and stitch all seam lines, leaving an opening unstitched between the small circles **(Figure N).**

3. Trim the seams to ¼ inch, clip corners and turn the suspenders right side out. Press, turning the unstitched seam allowance to the inside. Topstitch ¼ inch from all edges.

4. Sew 3 darts on the wrong side of each pants piece **(Figure O).** With right sides together sew the center pants seam, matching notches.

5. Turn the waist hem allowance to the inside, stitch, and press.

6. Place the suspenders over the Gork's shoulders, with the crosspiece in front. Cross the suspender straps in back and pin them in place.

7. Slip the pants over the lower body, tucking the suspenders inside. The long dart in the pants should be facing the front of the body. Add extra stuffing if necessary to fill out the pants. Hand stitch around the entire waistline to secure the pants to the shirt and suspenders.

Figure P

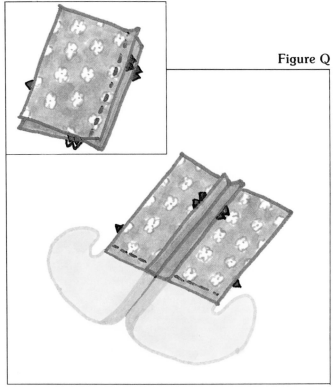

Figure Q

Figure R

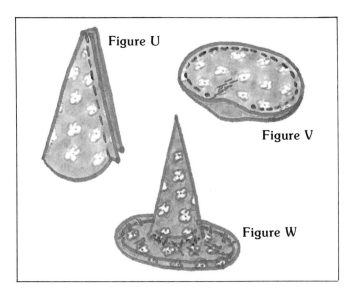

Figure S

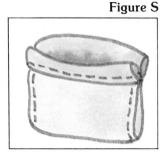

Figure T

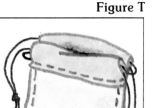

Figure U

Figure V

Figure W

Legs

1. Place 2 Leg pieces right sides together and sew the back leg seam **(Figure P)**. Press the seam open.

2. Place the Leg bottom and Foot top right sides together, and stitch **(Figure Q)**.

3. Sew the front leg seam and remaining foot seam **(Figure R)**. Clip curves, trim seams to ¼ inch, and turn right side out.

4. Turn the hem allowance on the leg to the inside and press. Do not stitch.

5. Repeat steps 1 through 4 for the remaining Leg and Foot pieces.

6. Firmly stuff both completed legs.

7. Pin the stuffed legs to the body at an angle as shown in the photograph. Hand stitch each leg to the body.

Herb bag

1. Turn the hem allowance on the herb bag to the wrong side and topstitch **(Figure S)**. Stitch both side seams up to the hem allowance. Do not stitch through the hem.

2. Turn the bag right side out and press.

3. Thread a length of narrow green ribbon through one hem, and back through the other hem. Leave about 4 inches of excess ribbon, and tie the ends in a knot **(Figure T)**. Repeat the process with a second length of ribbon, this time beginning at the opposite end of the hem. When completed, you will be able to pull the string ends to gather the top of the bag.

Hat

1. With right sides folded together, stitch the hat seam **(Figure U)**. Trim the seam to ¼ inch, and turn the hat right side out. Turn the hem allowance on the bottom to the wrong side and press. Topstitch ¼ inch from the edge.

2. Stitch the hat brim pieces right sides together, leaving an opening between the small circles **(Figure V)**. Clip the curves and trim the seams. Turn the hat brim right side out and press. Topstitch ¼ inch from the edge.

3. Center the hat on the hat brim. Blind stitch in place **(Figure W)**.

4. Hand tack the hat on the Gork's head.

Coiled Rug

This practical and affordable rug can be used in the entry hall, as an area rug in the living room, or as a cuddly mat in the bathroom.

Figure A

Materials

4 pairs of heavy "winter" pantyhose; 1 pair in each of the
    following colors: wine, navy, gray, and black.
1-inch-thick foam rubber 20 x 60 inches.
Heavy-duty thread and a long sharp needle.
3 yards of 3-inch-wide black fringe.
Scissors, iron, and sewing machine.
Yardstick and a soft pencil.

Making the rug

1. Cut the leg portions from 1 pair of pantyhose, eliminating all seams as shown in **Figure A.**

2. Cut each of the legs in half lengthwise so you now have 2 long flat pieces from each hose.

3. Repeat steps 1 and 2 for each of the remaining pairs of pantyhose.

80

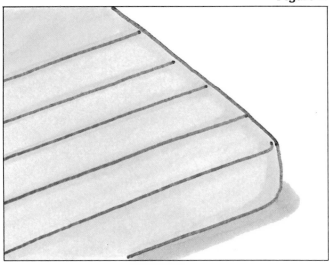

Figure B

4. Press each of the individual pieces lightly with a steam iron on low setting to remove as many wrinkles as possible.

5. Sew 2 wine-colored flat pieces together along 1 narrow end. Press the seam open.

6. Continue sewing the pieces together end to end, adding the wine first, then the gray, then blue, and finally black.

Cutting and sewing the coils

1. Use a yardstick and a soft pencil to mark off 1-inch-strips on the 1-inch-thick foam rubber **(Figure B)**. Mark carefully to make the strips as even as possible. Cut the strips apart along the marked lines.

2. Wrap the free end of hose around a foam rubber strip and sew a ¼-inch seam as shown in **Figure C.** When you reach the end of the strip, insert a second strip and continue stitching. Pull the hose only enough to stretch it over the strips. Keep the seam line evenly placed in the middle of one side. Do not allow the foam rubber strips to twist.

Finishing

1. Place the end of the hose-covered strips on a flat surface. Coil the strips in a circle around the end. As you work, be sure that you keep the coil flat and the seam hidden between the coils. Do not stretch the foam rubber inside the hose.

2. As you coil, whipstitch the upper edges of the coil together **(Figure D).**

3. When you reach the end, pull the foam rubber out of the hose enclosure. Cut the foam rubber at an angle as shown in **Figure E.** Replace the cut end of the foam rubber inside the hose and fold the hose over the end. Whipstitch the ends of the hose to the coiled rug.

4. Turn the rug over and place it on a flat surface. Whipstitch the coils together on the underside of the rug in the same manner as you did for the top.

5. Whipstitch 3-inch-wide black fringe securely around the outside of the rug.

Figure C

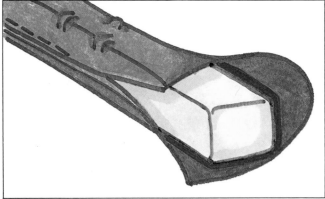

Figure D

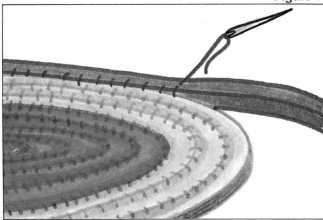

Figure E

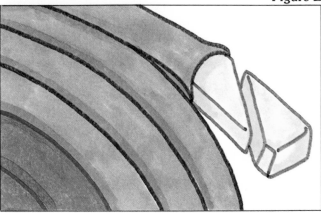

"Granny" & "Shady Lady"

These incredibly life-like characters may be the most enjoyable projects you have ever made. If you place them in a chair in your living room, they will watch over your home when you are not there, and may possibly scare off any uninvited guests.

Materials

To make 1 body:
> 7 pounds of polyester fiberfill
> 2 pairs of queen-size support pantyhose.
> 1 pair of regular pantyhose in a matching color.
> 1-inch diameter wooden dowel rod, 23 inches long.
> For the Shady Lady only, 1 additional leg of queen-size support pantyhose.

Purchased clothing (no larger than size 10) and shoes.
A wig and 2 empty egg-shaped pantyhose containers.
Costume jewelry.
False eyelashes.
False fingernails.
Powdered cheek blusher, brown and blue powdered eyeshadow, and a brown eyebrow pencil.
Red acrylic paint and a small paint brush (for Shady Lady's lips).
Scissors, glue, and straight pins.
Heavy-duty thread and a long sharp needle.
Clear fingernail polish.

Making the body

Although these 2 "ladies" have completely different personalities, the basic bodies are constructed the same.

1. 1 pair of queen-size support hose is used to make the legs and trunk. Stuff each leg with polyester fiberfill. Work from the toe up, keeping the 2 legs equal to each other in size. It is easier to work with a handful of fiberfill at a time. Keep the fiberfill as evenly distributed as possible. When finished, the legs should be approximately the same size as your own legs.

2. Continue stuffing the panty portion of the hose to form the trunk of the body **(Figure A)**. As you begin stuffing the trunk above the legs, place the hose on a chair to make sure that the completed character will bend at the top of the legs and sit correctly when finished.

3. After you have stuffed the hips, insert the wooden dowel rod in the center of the trunk. The rod will provide internal support for the finished figure and help to hold the head in place later.

4. When you have stuffed the waistline, slip the dress over the trunk and check the body size. If necessary, adjust the amount of stuffing to fit the dress. Remove the dress.

5. Continue to stuff the trunk, working around the center dowel rod and stretching the pantyhose up as you work. Be sure to add extra stuffing at the bust area. To fill out the bust, insert empty egg-shaped pantyhose containers on each side underneath a generous layer of fiberfill.

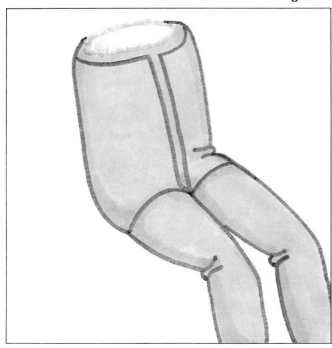

Figure A

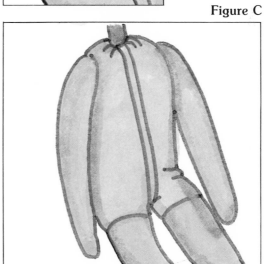

Figure B

Figure C

Figure D

6. When you have finished stuffing the trunk, the dowel rod should project about 6 inches above the trunk in the center of the neckline **(Figure B)**.

7. Baste ¼ inch from the edge around the neckline opening using heavy-duty thread. Pull the gathering thread to close the opening around the dowel rod at the neck.

8. Cut 2 legs from queen-size support pantyhose and stuff them to form the arms. Keep the arms as equal in size as possible. When stuffed, the arms should be approximately the same size and length as your own arm. Tie a knot in the hose at the top of the arm.

9. Position the arms at a slight angle to the shoulders. Use heavy-duty thread and a needle to whipstitch the arms to the body **(Figure C)**.

Making the head

1. To form the head, tie a knot at the panty line of 1 leg of regular pantyhose. Cut 1 inch above the knot. Cut again 14 inches below the knot. Turn the hose so the knot is on the inside.

2. Stuff generous amounts of fiberfill inside the hose, manipulating the shape until a head is formed **(Figure D)**. Push the fiberfill evenly toward the hose so that your hand forms a cavity inside the head. To shape the head, add fiberfill inside the cavity. This will keep the fiberfill layer around the outside smooth and even. The completed head should be approximtely the same size as your own. Tie the hose together loosely at the neck with string. The string will later be untied to insert the dowel rod.

Figure F

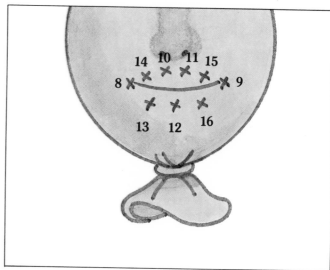

3. Use a long sharp needle and heavy-duty thread to form the nose. Follow the entry and exit points illustrated in **Figure E.**

    a. Enter at 1 and exit at 2. Pinch up a vertical ridge in the center of the face. Stitch back and forth under the ridge, exiting at 3.

    b. Use the tip of the needle to carefully lift the fiberfill along the ridge. Gently pull the thread and lock the stitch.

    c. To form the nostrils, reenter at 3 and exit at 4.

    d. Reenter ¼ inch above 4 and exit at 3.

    e. Reenter at 3 and exit at 5.

    f. Reenter at 5 and exit at 6.

    g. Reenter ¼ inch above 6 and exit at 7. Pull the thread and lock the stitch under the bridge of the nose.

4. Continue working with the same thread to form the mouth.

    a. Reenter at 7 and exit at 8.

    b. Pull the thread across the surface, enter at 9 and exit at 3.

    c. Pull the thread until a smile appears. Reenter at 3 and exit at 7.

    d. Lock the stitch and cut the thread.

5. On Granny only, add additional stitches to the mouth, following the entry and exit points given in **Figure F.**

    a. Enter at 8 and exit at 10.

    b. Reenter at 10 and exit at 11.

    c. Reenter at 11 and exit at 12. Pull the thread to form the lips. Lock the stitch.

    d. Reenter at 12 and exit at 13.

    e. Reenter at 13 and exit at 14.

    f. Reenter at 14 and exit at 15.

    g. Reenter at 15 and exit at 16.

    h. Reenter at 16 and exit at 12. Pull the thread very gently. Lock the stitch and cut the thread.

6. Brush powdered cheek blusher on the cheek and across the bottom lip.

Figure E

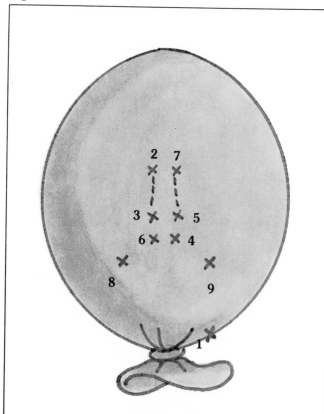

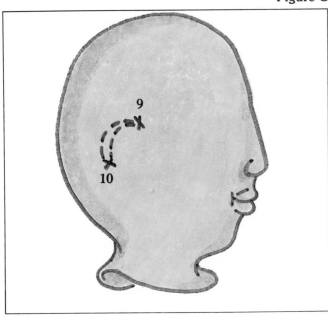

Figure G

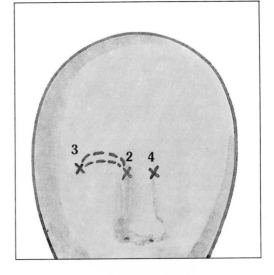

Figure H

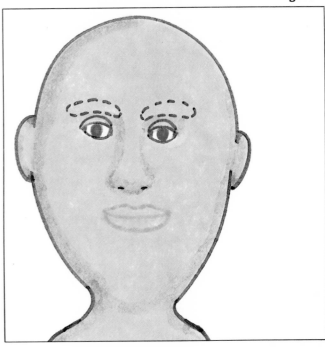

Figure I

7. To form the ears, follow the entry and exit points illustrated in **Figure G.**

    a. Pinch up a small ridge at an angle on the side of the head just below the eye line. Enter at 1 and exit at 9.

    b. Stitch under the ridge back and forth until an ear forms. Exit at 10.

    c. Lock the stitch and return to 1.

    d. Lock the stitch and cut the thread.

8. Repeat step 7 on the other side of the head.

9. To form the eyes and eyelids, follow the entry and exit points illustrated in **Figure H.**

    a. Enter at 1 and exit at 2.

    b. Enter at 3 and exit at 2. Pull the thread and lock the stitch.

    c. Pinch up a narrow curved ridge over the left eye.

    d. Reenter at 2 and stitch back and forth under the ridge, exiting at 3.

    e. Reenter at 3 and exit at 2. Pull the thread and lock the stitch.

    f. Reenter at 2 and exit at 4.

10. Repeat the procedures in step 9 (b through 3) on the right side of the face to form the other eye and eyelid.

11. Paint the eyes using acrylic paint and a small paint brush. Paint the entire eye sockets with white paint. Let the paint dry. Paint blue eyeballs in the center of the white sockets.

12. To form Granny's eyebrows, pinch up a larger ridge over the eyelids even with the top of the nose, and stitch back and forth underneath the ridge **(Figure I).**

Figure L

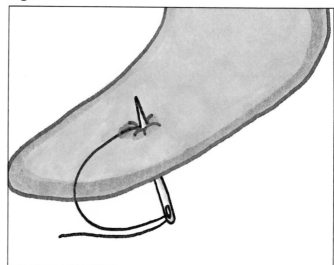

Figure J

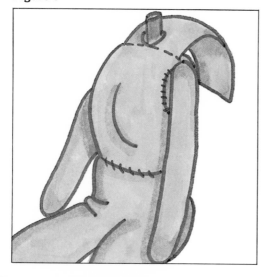

Figure K

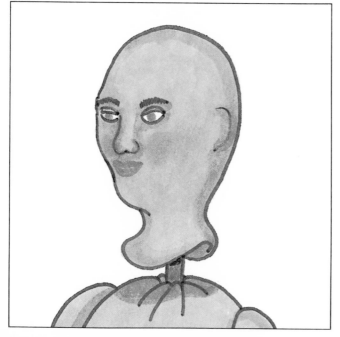

Forming the Shady Lady's neckline

1. Forming the low neckline for the Shady Lady requires additional steps before adding the head. Cut 1 leg from a pair of pantyhose at the panty line.

2. Cut the hose leg up 1 side and open it out flat.

3. Cover the top portion of the trunk with a thick layer of polyester fiberfill. Begin just under the bust line and end at the center back.

4. Whipstitch one end of the flat hose across the trunk just under the bust line, stretching the hose to fit from side to side. Whipstitch the edges of the hose to the trunk under the arm, around the armholes, and at the top of the shoulder **(Figure J)**.

5. Stretch the center of the hose up to the neckline to determine where the dowel rod will fit. Mark the position on the hose. Paint a 2-inch diameter circle with clear nail polish and let it dry. Cut out the center of the circle to a size large enough to accommodate the wood dowel rod.

6. Stretch the remaining portion of the hose leg to the center back, whipstitching it in place as you did for the front.

Attaching the head

1. Untie the string on the neck and center the head over the dowel rod in the neckline opening. Force the rod into the cavity in the center of the head **(Figure K)**.

2. Carefully whipstitch completely around the neck several times to secure the head to the body.

Feet

1. Insert the needle 1½ inches from the top of the foot. This will be the base of the first toe.

2. Wrap the thread around the end of the foot. Enter the needle on the bottom of the foot and exit on top of the foot where you began **(Figure L)**.

3. Pull the thread tightly to form 1 toe. Lock the stitch.

4. Reenter at the point where you just exited. Take a ½-inch stitch under the surface and exit at the base of the second toe **(Figure M)**.

5. Repeat steps 2 through 4 four more times to form the remaining toes.

6. Bend the foot into an L-shape at the ankle **(Figure N)**. Whipstitch the top of the foot to the front of the ankle and pull the thread tightly. Lock the stitch and cut the thread.

Hands

1. Use the same basic technique to form the hands that you used to shape the toes. Follow the entry and exit points illustrated in **Figure O.**

> **a.** Insert the needle on the underside, 5 inches from the end of the left hand. This will be the base of the thumb.
>
> **b.** Pinch up a ridge on the thumb side of the hand. Enter at 2 and exit on the underside.
>
> **c.** Wrap the thread around what will be the end of the thumb to the front of the hand. Enter at 2 and exit at 1.
>
> **d.** Pull the thread and lock the stitch. Reenter at 1 and exit at 3.
>
> **e.** Stitch up and down through the hand along the dotted line between 3 and 4.
>
> **f.** Enter at 4 and exit at 5. Pull the thread and lock the stitch.
>
> **g.** To form the last 3 fingers, repeat the procedure, stitching between 5 and 6 and then between 7 and 8.
>
> **h.** Lock the last stitch and cut the thread.

2. Rethread the needle and enter at 1. Push the needle through the hand and enter on the bottom of the wrist.

3. Wrap the thread around the outside of the wrist. Lock the stitch and cut the thread.

Finishing

1. Make up the face exactly as you would your own. The Shady Lady's eyebrows are drawn on with an eyebrow pencil and her mouth is painted with a small paint brush and red acrylic paint.

2. On Granny, use a brown eyebrow pencil to draw crow's-feet at the corner of her eyes, and add lines from the sides of her nose to the sides of the mouth.

3. Dress the completed doll and add any jewelry you wish. Arrange the wig to your liking, and glue it to the top of the head.

4. Glue false eyelashes to the eyelids and false fingernails to the tips of the fingers.

5. Put shoes on the feet. Glue or sew the shoes to the feet if necessary to hold them in place.

Figure M

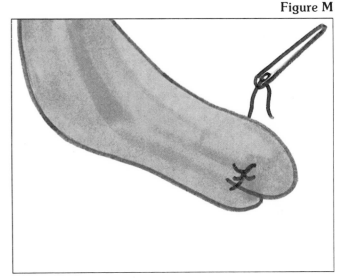

Figure N

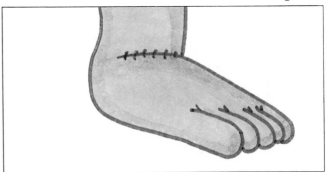

Figure O

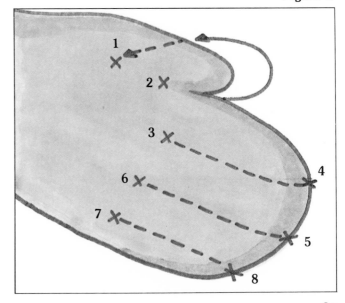

Pantyhose Cactus

This fool-the-eye cactus plant is sure to be a conversation piece. And it requires even less care than a real one!

Figure A

Materials

1 leg of nurse's white pantyhose.
1 leg of brown opaque knee-high hose.
1 lid from an aerosol spray can.
¼ pound of polyester fiberfill.
Heavy-duty clear nylon thread and a long sharp needle.
Green spray paint.
Ceramic container (or other planter).
Scissors.

Making the cactus

1. To make the cactus, tie a knot at the panty line on 1 leg of pantyhose. Cut 1 inch above the knot. Cut again 8 inches below the knot. Turn the hose so the knot is on the inside.

2. Stuff the hose with polyester fiberfill to form an elongated sphere about 6 inches long and 3½ inches in diameter (**Figure A**). Tie a knot in the hose at the bottom.

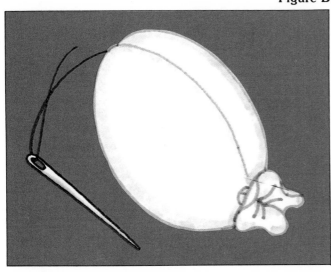

Figure B

Figure C

3. Use a needle and heavy-duty thread to section the cactus **(Figure B)**.

    a. Insert the needle at the center bottom of the cactus.

    b. Pull the thread up the outside and enter the needle at the center top of the cactus. Pull the thread to form a groove. Lock the stitch to hold it in place.

    c. Pull the thread down the opposite side of the cactus and insert the needle through the knot at the bottom. Pull the thread to form a groove, and lock the stitch.

4. Repeat step 3 three more times to complete the sectioning. Lock the last stitch.

Finishing the cactus

1. Use a long sharp needle and heavy-duty thread to form the cactus needles **(Figure C)**. Take a stitch and pull both ends of the thread to 3 inches long. Tie the 2 ends in a double knot. Cut both threads to ¾ inch long.

2. Repeat step 1 until the cactus is covered with needles.

3. Tie a piece of string around the knot in the bottom of the cactus. Hang the cactus upside down and spray paint it green. Allow the paint to dry completely.

Making the potting soil

1. Cut the ribbed portion from a brown knee-high hose.

2. Stretch the ribbed hose over the aerosol can lid so the raw edges of the hose are on the bottom and the ribbed top closes in over the open portion of the lid **(Figure D)**.

3. Gather the cut edges of the hose on the bottom of the lid using a needle and heavy-duty thread. Pull the gathering threads only enough to hold the hose together flat against the bottom of the lid.

Figure D

Figure F

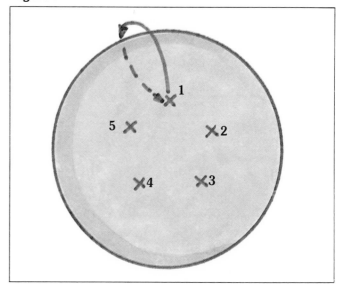

4. To "plant" the cactus, stretch the top of the hose open, insert the cactus, and allow the hose top to close back around it and hold it in place **(Figure E)**.

5. Place the potted cactus inside the container of your choice.

Adding the cactus bloom

1. To make the cactus bloom, form a small ball of polyester fiberfill and wrap it with a 2-inch-diameter piece cut from regular pantyhose. Gather the raw edges of the hose together and tie them with thread.

2. Flatten the ball so the gathers are on the underside. Follow the illustrations given in **Figure F** to form the bloom. Use a long sharp needle and heavy-duty thread.

   a. Enter on the back at the gathered area and exit at 1.

   b. Wrap the thread around the edge to the back. Enter behind 1 and exit at 1 again.

   c. Enter at 2 and exit on the back.

   d. Wrap the thread around the edge to the front. Enter at 2 and exit on the back.

   e. Reenter on the back and exit at 2.

   f. Enter at 3 and exit on the back.

   g. Wrap the thread around the edge to the front. Enter at 3 and exit on the back.

   h. Reenter on the back and exit at 3.

   i. Enter at 4 and exit on the back.

   j. Wrap the thread around the edge to the front. Enter at 4 and exit on the back.

   k. Enter on the back and exit at 4.

   l. Enter at 5 and exit on the back.

   m. Wrap the thread around the edge to the front. Enter at 5 and exit on the back.

   n. Reenter on the back and exit at 5.

   o. Enter at 1 and exit on the back. Lock the stitch and cut the thread.

3. Hand tack the bloom to the top of the cactus plant.

Figure E

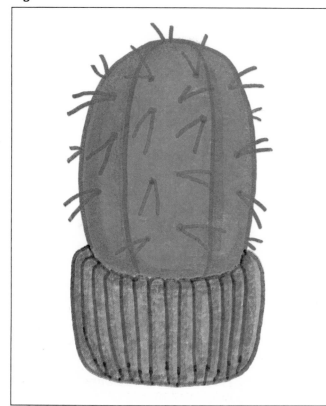

Sculptured Head

You can make this expensive-looking art object yourself using a new technique with pantyhose. When finished, it looks and feels like a solid ceramic sculpture.

Figure A

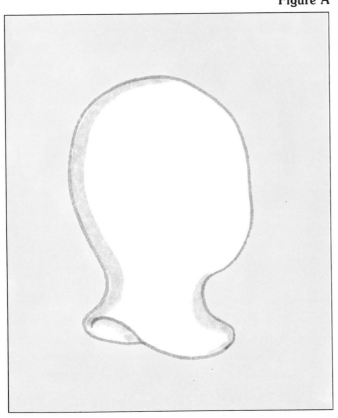

Materials

1 pair of nurse's white pantyhose.
White acrylic spray paint.
Acrylic gesso (available from most art and hobby stores).
Small paint brush.
White fiber.
½ pound of polyester fiberfill.
Heavy-duty white thread, scissors, and a long sharp needle.
12-inch-length of ⅜-inch-diameter wooden dowel rod.
4 x 6-inch piece of wood, 2 inches thick with a ⅜-inch hole drilled in the center.
Glue.

Making the head

1.   To form the head, tie a knot at the panty line on 1 leg of white pantyhose. Cut 1 inch above the knot. Cut off the toe seam. Turn the hose so the knot is on the inside.

2.   Stuff generous amounts of fiberfill inside the hose, manipulating the shape until a head is formed **(Figure A).** The head should be about life size. Push the fiberfill evenly toward the hose so that your hand forms a cavity inside the head. Add fiberfill inside the cavity to shape the head. This will keep the fiberfill next to the hose smooth and even.

Figure C

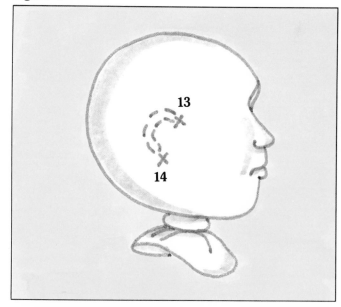

Figure B

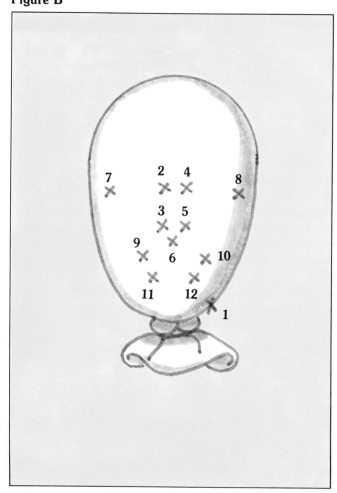

3. When the head is shaped, remove your hand and stuff the cavity with additional amounts of fiberfill.

4. Tie a knot in the hose at the neck.

5. Use a long sharp needle and heavy-duty thread to form the facial features. Follow the entry and exit points illustrated in **Figure B.**

  a. Enter at 1 and exit at 2.

  b. Enter at 3 and exit at 4.

  c. Enter at 5 and exit at 6.

  d. Enter at 5 and exit at 3.

  e. Enter at 6 and exit at 2.

  f. Pull the thread tightly, and lock the stitch under the bridge of the nose.

  g. Pinch up a ridge across the brow line. Stitch back and forth under the ridge, exiting at 7.

  h. Enter at 2 and exit at 4.

  i. Pinch up a ridge across the other brow line. Stitch back and forth under the ridge, exiting at 8.

  j. Enter at 4 and exit at 2. Pull the thread tightly and lock the stitch.

  k. Reenter at 2 and exit between 5 and 6.

  l. Reenter between 5 and 6 and exit at 2. Pull the thread and lock the stitch.

  m. Enter at 2 and exit at 4.

  n. Reenter at 4 and exit between 3 and 6.

  o. Reenter between 3 and 6 and exit at 4. Pull the thread and lock the stitch.

  p. Reenter at 4 and exit at 9.

  q. Enter at 10 and exit at 2. Pull the thread and lock the stitch.

  r. Reenter at 2 and exit at 11.

  s. Enter at 12 and exit at 4. Pull the thread and lock the stitch.

  t. Reenter at 4 and exit at 1. Lock the stitch and cut the thread.

6. Use the tip of the needle to raise the cheeks and nose.

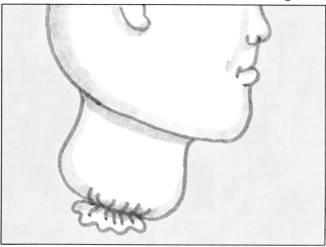

Figure D

5. To make the ears, follow the entry and exit points illustrated in **Figure C.**

 a. Pinch up a small ridge at an angle on the side of the head just below the eye line. Enter at 1 and exit at 13.

 b. Stitch under the ridge back and forth until an ear forms. Exit at 14.

 c. Lock the stitch and return to 1.

 d. Lock the stitch and trim the thread.

6. Repeat step 5 on the other side of the head to form the other ear.

The neck and hair

1. Stuff the hose under the knot to form the neck. When complete, the neck should measure approximately 6 inches in diameter and 4 inches long.

2. Gather the hose under the neck using a needle and heavy-duty thread **(Figure D)**. Pull the gathers together, leaving a ½-inch diameter hole in the center. Tie the threads in a knot.

3. Cut off the excess hose beneath the gathers and push the gathers inside the center of the neck.

4. Insert the dowel rod through the hole in the center of the gathers and push it firmly up inside the head.

5. Place the other end of the dowel rod inside the hole drilled in the center of the wood block.

6. Wrap white fiber around the head, gluing it in place as shown in **Figure E**. Use heavy-duty thread and a needle to stitch over the fiber to form a side part.

Finishing

1. Tape newspapers securely around the dowel rod underneath the neck. Spray paint the head with white paint. Allow the paint to dry overnight.

2. Brush 2 coats of gesso over the painted head, allowing the first coat to dry thoroughly before adding the second one.

3. Allow the completed head to dry overnight.

Figure E

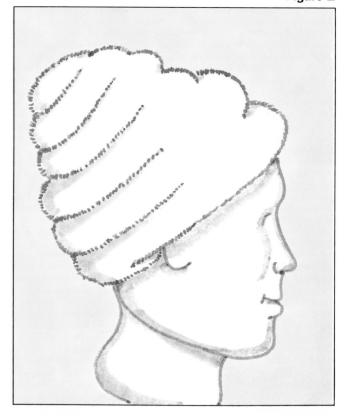

Snow Dove

This snowy white dove is an eye-catching decorator accent for either a live green plant or an artificial arrangement. You can also use it to adorn a door wreath or at the base of a Christmas candle.

Figure A

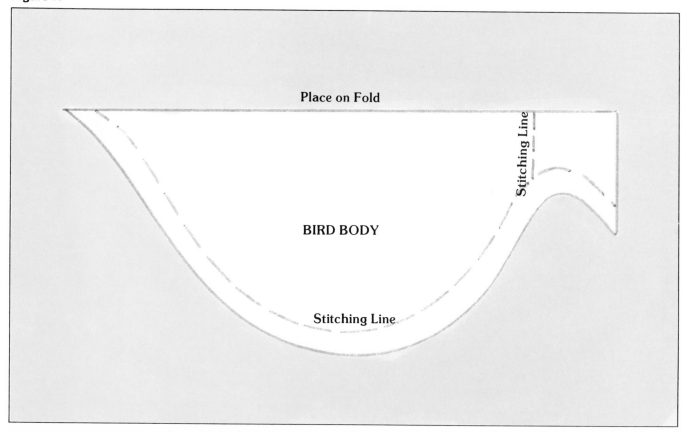

Place on Fold

Stitching Line

BIRD BODY

Stitching Line

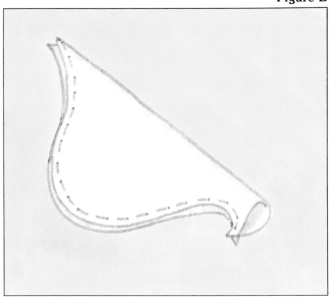

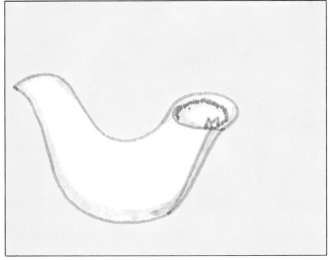

Figure C

Materials

1 leg of nurse's white pantyhose.
¼ pound of polyester fiberfill.
Heavy-duty white thread and a long sharp needle.
Grapevine bird's nest and artificial foliage.
Scissors, glue, black laundry marker, and white sewing thread.
Yellow acrylic paint and a small paint brush.
Tracing paper and a pencil.

Making the bird

1. Cut the toe section from a leg of white pantyhose 4 inches above the toe seam. Set it aside for later use in making the tail.

2. A full-size pattern for the bird Body is given in **Figure A**. Trace the pattern using tracing paper and a pencil.

3. Cut a 10-inch section of hose from the remaining portion of the pantyhose leg. Place the full-size pattern on the hose, positioning the straight pattern edge on the fold, and cut it out.

4. Stitch the body together, leaving the tail open to allow for turning and stuffing **(Figure B)**.

5. Turn the body right side out. Stuff the body with polyester fiberfill, working through the opening in the tail. Stuff the beak very lightly. Refer to the illustration in **Figure C** to shape the body. As you stuff, keep the sewn seam at the center bottom of the body.

6. After the body is stuffed, flatten the tail across the back and sew across the stitching line to close the opening **(Figure D)**.

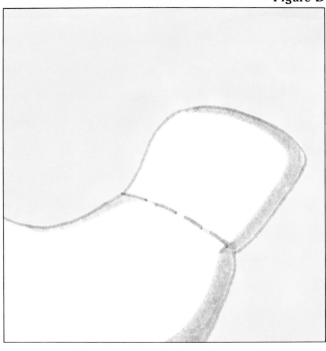

Figure E

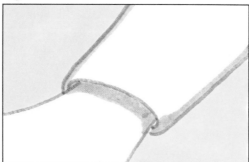

Figure F

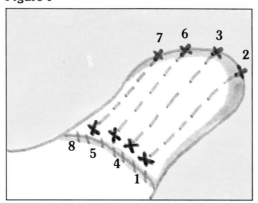

Figure G

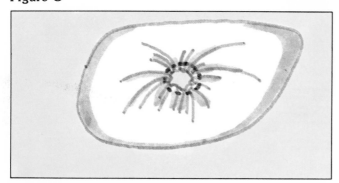

Figure H

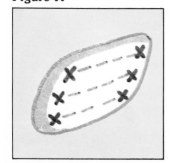

Figure I

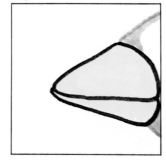

Making the tail

1. To make the tail, stuff the 4-inch toe section of pantyhose that you set aside earlier. When stuffed, it should measure 3½ inches long and 2½ inches wide.

2. Turn the raw edges to the inside and fit the stuffed tail over the stitching on the bird's body. Whipstitch the folded edges of the tail over the stitching line **(Figure E)**.

3. Use a needle and heavy-duty thread to section the tail, following the entry and exit points illustrated in **(Figure F)**.

    a. Enter the needle on the underside of the tail and exit at 1.

    b. Backstitch along the dotted line between 1 and 2. Exit at 2.

    c. Wrap the thread around the end of the tail to the underside. Enter under 2 and exit at 2.

    d. Reenter at 2 and exit at 3.

    e. Wrap the thread around the end of the tail to the underside. Enter under 3 and exit at 3.

    f. Backstitch along the stitching line between 3 and 4, exiting at 4.

    g. Reenter at 4 and exit at 5.

    h. Complete the tail by backstitching the remaining 2 lines, between points 5 and 6 and then points 7 and 8, as illustrated in Figure F.

    i. Lock the stitch and cut the thread.

Making the wings

1. To make the wing, form a ball of polyester fiberfill 2 inches in diameter. Wrap the fiberfill with a 4-inch-diameter circle cut from white pantyhose. Gather the raw edges of the hose together and tie them with thread.

2. Flatten the ball so the gathers are on the underside. Pull opposite sides of the circle to shape the wing **(Figure G)**.

3. Backstitch 3 rows on the wing in the same manner used on the tail **(Figure H)**.

4. Repeat steps 1 through 3 to make the other wing.

5. Whipstitch the completed wings to each side of the bird's body.

Finishing

1. Paint the beak portion of the body yellow using a small paint brush. Let the paint dry.

2. Dot a black eye on each side of the bird's head using a laundry marker.

4. Line the beak lightly with a black laundry marker as shown in **Figure I.**

5. Arrange the completed dove and artificial foliage in a grapevine basket.

Footstool

A whimsical creation that will charm children and adults alike.

Materials

1 pair of regular pantyhose.
2 pairs of blue opaque knee-high hose.
1 yard of ¾-inch-wide brightly striped ribbon.
1 pair of men's shoes with laces.
½ pound of polyester fiberfill.
Blue sewing thread and a needle.
Scissors and glue.
Staple gun and staples.
For the wooden inner support:
      13 x 26-inch piece of ½-inch-thick plywood.
      20-inch length of 2 x 2-inch lumber.
      Pencil, saw, 1½-inch wood screws, and carpenter's
         wood glue.

Making the inner support

1. Cut a 13-inch-diameter circle of plywood for the footstool top.

2. Cut a pair of plywood "feet" to fit inside the shoes. The easiest method is to have the person who wears the shoes stand on the plywood, and then trace around his feet.

3. Cut the 20-inch length of 2 x 2 lumber in half lengthwise to form two 10-inch-long "legs".

Figure A

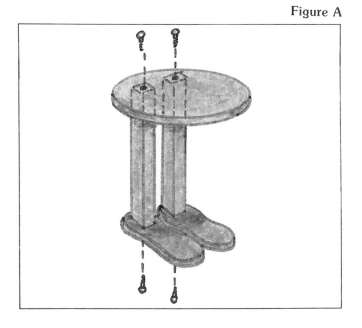

4. Assemble the inner support for the footstool using both glue and screws, as shown in **Figure A**. The "legs" should be positioned about 2 inches from the heel of the foot to provide maximum stability for the finished footstool. Let the glue dry overnight.

Figure D

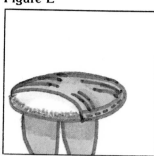

Figure E

Figure B

Figure F

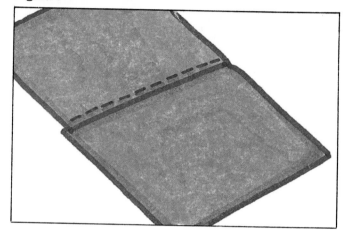

Figure C

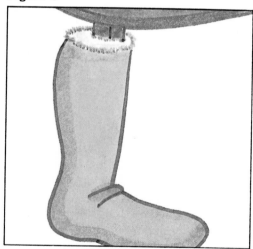

5. Cut 2 legs from a pair of pantyhose at the panty line.

6. Gather 1 leg of hose up to the toe (as if you were going to put it on) and slip it over the toe of the wooden foot. Stuff polyester fiberfill inside the hose on top of the wooden foot to plump it out **(Figure B)**.

7. Continue to pull the hose over the foot and leg, stuffing with fiberfill as you work. Stuff the front of the leg only enough to round it out. The main portion of the stuffing should be at the back of the leg so that it fills out even with the heel of the foot **(Figure C)**.

8. Continue to stuff the leg to the top of the footstool. At the top, release the hose and it will curl over the leg stuffing.

9. Repeat steps 6 through 8 to stuff the remaining leg. As you work, keep the second leg the same size and shape as the first.

Finishing the legs

1. Pull a pair of navy knee-high hose over the feet and roll them down to just above the ankles.

2. Slip the shoes over the feet, and lace them up.

Upholstering the top

1. Cover the top of the footstool with an even layer of polyester fiberfill approximately 1 inch thick.

2. Use the remaining portion of the pantyhose to cut an inner cover for the footstool top. Cut out 1 side of the panty portion (between the front and back seams) as shown in **Figure D**.

3. Carefully place the hose over the fiberfill padding. Staple the hose to the front edge of the wooden top. Stretch the hose over the padding and staple it to the back edge **(Figure E)**. Staple the sides next, and then staple the remaining edges.

4. Cut the ribbed section and the toe seam from 2 navy opaque knee-high hose. Cut along 1 side and open each hose out flat.

5. Place the 2 flat hose pieces together and sew along 1 long side **(Figure F)**. Stretch the hose gently as you stitch to retain the elasticity.

6. Cover the footstool with the blue hose using the same procedure as for the inner cover (Step 3).

7. Glue the striped ribbon around the stapled edges, beginning and ending at the back of the footstool.

Magical Unicorn

Unicorns are very special animals that spread their magic wherever they go. Just looking at him, it's hard to believe that he is made from cardboard and nurse's white pantyhose.

2 pairs of nurse's white support hose.
2 ounces of yellow fiber.
¾ yard of gold metallic stretch cording.
2 pounds of polyester fiberfill.
2 small black beads.
12-inch square of black felt.
1 yard of 1-inch-wide white seam binding.
12 x 20-inch piece of heavy cardboard.
2 small black feathers (or a pair of purchased eyelashes).
1 yard of 1-inch-wide ribbon.
Heavy-duty white nylon thread, glue, straight pins, scissors, powdered cheek blusher, and a long sharp needle.
Pencil and paper to enlarge the patterns.

Making the body

1. Enlarge the patterns given in **Figure A** to full size. Cut the full-size unicorn body out of heavy cardboard.

2. Glue a layer of fiberfill around the raw edges of the cardboard body, as shown in **Figure B.**

3. Cut 1 leg from the pantyhose at the panty line.

4. Gather the leg in your hands up to the toe (as if you were going to put it on) and ease the leg over the cardboard nose. Stretch the leg over the body, working out the wrinkles and positioning the leg opening at the rear of the body **(Figure C).**

5. Stuff 1 side of the body using a handful of fiberfill at a time. Work from the tip of the nose to the rear opening. Repeat the stuffing procedure for the remaining side of the body.

6. Gather the open end of the hose using a needle and heavy white nylon thread. Pull the thread to close the opening and lock the stitches. Trim off the excess hose with scissors.

Constructing the legs

1. Cut 2 legs from the pantyhose at the panty line. Cut off both feet at the ankle **(Figure D).**

2. Carefully cut each hose lengthwise and open it out flat. Cut lengthwise down the center, making 2 equal pieces from each hose (a total of 4 pieces).

Figure A

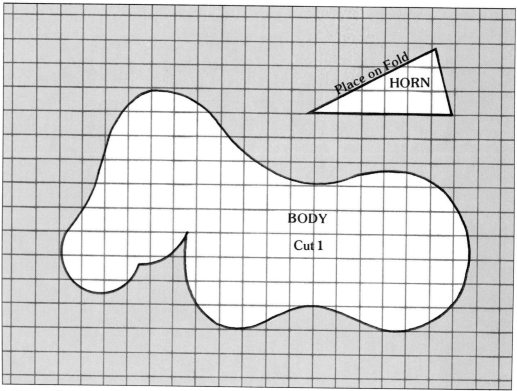

Place on Fold

HORN

BODY

Cut 1

Figure B

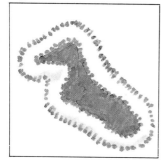

Figure C

Figure D

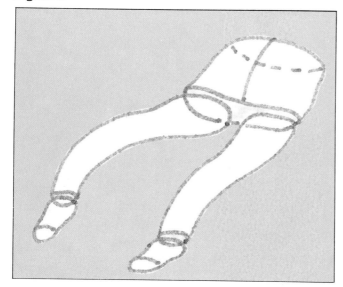

3. Fold 1 piece in half lengthwise and machine stitch down the long open side and across the end to form a long tube **(Figure E).** Stretch the pantyhose gently as you sew to retain the elasticity of the hose. Repeat for the other 3 pieces.

4. Turn all 4 stitched tubes right side out and stuff each of them to form the legs. Stuff the bottom of the tube until the leg is approximately 2 inches in diameter. Approximately 6 inches from the open end, begin overstuffing to form the rear haunches and front shoulders **(Figure F).** The 2 front shoulders should be approximately 5 inches in diameter and the 2 rear haunches should be about 6 inches in diameter.

5. Fold the raw edges on the open end of the tube to one side, and whipstitch flat as shown in **Figure G.**

6. Whipstitch the 4 legs to the body, placing the whipstitched raw edges next to the body, as shown in **Figure H.** Make certain that the 2 smaller front shoulders are positioned at the front, and the larger rear haunches are at the back.

7. Cut a 1-inch-wide length of black felt and glue it around one "hoof." Cut a black circle of felt to fit the bottom of the "hoof," and glue it in place. Repeat the procedure for each hoof.

Making the horn

1. Cut the horn from one of the remaining hose feet, placing the pattern edge marked "place on fold" on the bottom of the hose foot **(Figure I).** Gently stretching the hose, stitch the horn from top to bottom. Turn the hose right side out.

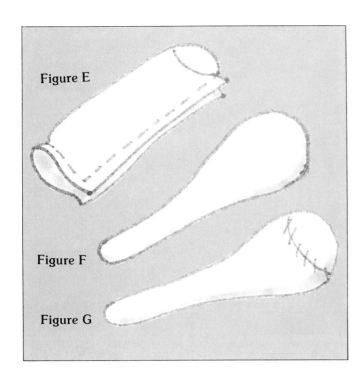

Figure E

Figure F

Figure G

Figure H

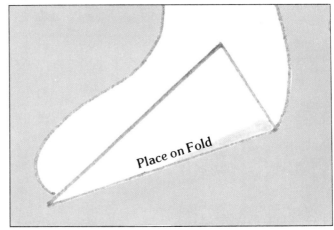

Figure I

Place on Fold

2. Stuff the horn evenly from tip to opening, keeping it as round as possible. Gather the opening with needle and heavy-duty thread.

3. Hand stitch the horn to the forehead (refer to the photograph for placement). Lock the stitch and pull the thread up around the horn toward the tip to form a twisted effect (**Figure J**). Pull the thread tightly and lock the stitch at the tip of the horn.

4. Securely stitch 1 end of the gold stretch cord at the base of the horn. Twist the cord around the horn following the indentations formed by the thread. Stitch the cord in place at the tip of the horn.

Forming the ears, eyes, nose, and mouth

1. Cut two 4-inch-diameter circles from 1 of the remaining hose feet.

2. Gently stretch 1 hose circle around a 3-inch-diameter ball of fiberfill to form an ear. Crease 1 side with your finger and gently pull the top of the ear to form a point (**Figure K**). Tie the raw edges together with thread.

3. Whipstitch the ears to the top of the head, hiding the raw edges.

Figure J

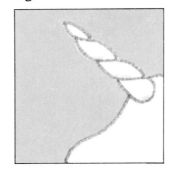

Figure K

Figure L

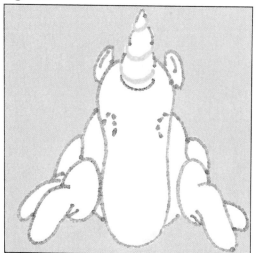

Figure M

Figure N

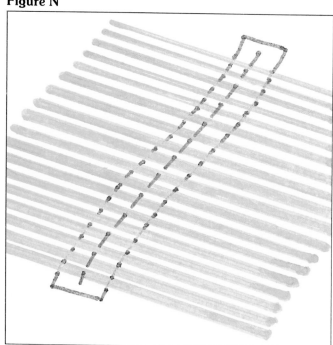

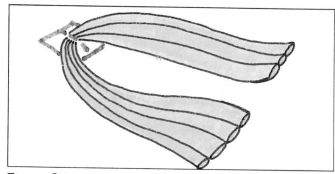

Figure O

Mane and tail

4. Draw 2 equally spaced half-circles on either side of the face, 2½ inches down from the base of the horn **(Figure L)**.

5. Pinch up a ridge under each of the half-circles and stitch back and forth under the ridge with heavy-duty thread to shape an eyelid. Take 1 long stitch beneath the eyelid to pull the opposite ends together in a gentle curve. Lock the stitch.

6. Glue the black beads beneath the eyelids. Trim the feathers to eyelash size and glue them in place (or substitute actual false eyelashes).

7. To form the nostrils, repeat the eyelid process (steps 4 and 5) on either side of the muzzle.

8. Push the end of the muzzle inward and stitch across the indentation to form the mouth **(Figure M)**. Brush powdered cheek blusher on the lips.

1. Cut 7-inch lengths of fiber or yarn for the mane. Center them across a 9-inch-long strip of white seam binding **(Figure N)**. Machine stitch carefully down the center through the fiber and seam binding.

2. Glue or hand stitch the mane to the center back, beginning just behind the horn.

3. Stitch a generous amount of 12-inch-long fiber or yarn to a 1-inch-square piece of seam binding to form the tail **(Figure O)**. Stitch or glue the seam binding to the body to cover the hose knot at the rear of the unicorn.

4. Trim the mane and tail to the desired length. The fiber can be twisted and glued in place to form curls. If you use yarn, untwist each strand.

5. Tie a ribbon bow and whipstitch it to the top of the tail.

CELEBRATIONS

...sparkling additions

to special occasions

Halloween Ghost & Pumpkin

Use these Halloween characters to decorate a party table or combine them with a branch of fall leaves to hang on the door.

Materials

To make the ghost:
    1 pair of nurse's white pantyhose.
    A scrap piece of black felt.
    5-inch long white paper tube cut from a tissue roll.
To make the pumpkin:
    1 leg cut from a pair of regular pantyhose.
    2 small black buttons.
    Scrap pieces of brown and green felt.
    Black felt-tip marker and scotch tape.
    Orange acrylic spray paint.
    Tracing paper and a pencil.
A small amount of polyester fiberfill.
Heavy-duty clear nylon thread and a long sharp needle.
Scissors and glue.

Making the ghost
The body and head

1. Cut the toe from 1 leg of white pantyhose, 6 inches above the bottom seam.

2. Cut a 5-inch cardboard tube and insert it in the hose. Tuck the raw edges of the hose inside the top of the tube, and glue them in place **(Figure A)**.

3. To form the ghost's head, cut a circle of hose 4 inches in diameter. Form a ball of fiberfill 3 inches in diameter. Wrap the hose circle around the fiberfill. Gather the raw edges of the hose at the bottom of the head and tie them together with thread.

Figure A

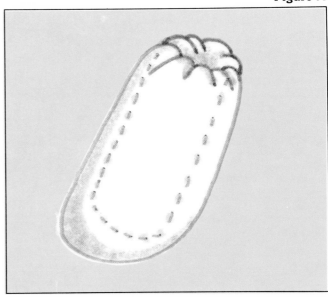

Figure D

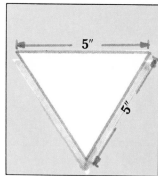

5"
5"

Figure E

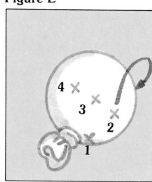

4 ✕
3 ✕
2 ✕
1 ✕

Figure B

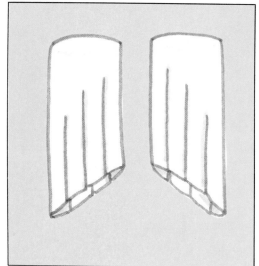

Figure F

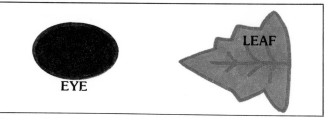

EYE

LEAF

Figure G

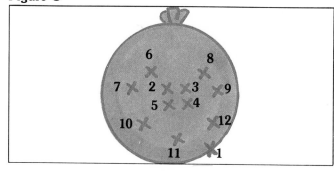

6 ✕
8 ✕
7 ✕ 2 ✕ 3 ✕ 9 ✕
5 ✕ 4 ✕
10 ✕ 12 ✕
11 ✕ 1 ✕

Figure C

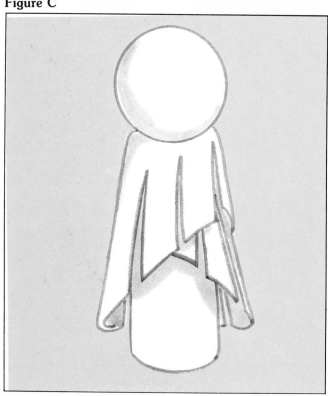

4. Glue the head to the top of the hose-covered tube.

5. Cut an 8-inch length of white hose. Cut the hose in half diagonally. Cut every ½ inch along the diagonal edges to fringe both halves (**Figure B**).

6. Gather the straight raw edges of each half using heavy-duty clear nylon thread.

7. Slip the fringed halves over the head. Pull the gathering threads to fit around the neckline (**Figure C**). Tuck the gathers in place. Glue the gathers to the tube around the neckline.

8. Cut a triangular piece of hose to the dimensions specified in **Figure D**. Cut fringe along the 2 short edges, and wrap it around the head. Glue it in place.

The hands and eyes

1. To make 1 hand, form a small ball of polyester fiberfill and wrap it with a 2-inch-diameter circle of white hose. Gather the raw edges of the hose at the bottom of the ball and tie them together with thread.

2. Use heavy-duty thread and a long sharp needle to form the fingers. Follow the entry and exit points given in **Figure E.**

    a. Insert the needle at 1 and exit at 2.

    b. Pull the thread around the ball (on the surface), enter behind 2 and exit at 2.

    c. Pull the thread tightly and lock the stitch.

    d. Reenter at 2, take a ¼-inch stitch underneath the surface, exiting at 3.

    e. Pull the thread around the back, enter behind 3 and exit at 3.

    f. Repeat the steps b through c at point 4 to form the last 2 fingers.

3. Repeat steps 1 and 2 to make the other hand. Glue both hands underneath the chin.

4. Cut 2 black felt oval eyes and glue them to the ghost's face. A full-size pattern is given in **Figure F.**

Making the pumpkin
The head

1. To form the pumpkin head, tie a knot at the panty line on a pantyhose leg. Cut 1 inch above the knot. Cut again 10 inches below the knot. Turn the hose so the knot is on the inside.

2. Stuff generous amounts of fiberfill inside the hose until it is round and full. It should measure approximately 15 inches in circumference. Tie the hose in a knot at the top.

3. Use a long sharp needle and heavy-duty thread to form the nose. Follow the entry and exit points illustrated in **Figure G.**

    a. Enter at 1 and exit at 2.

    b. Enter at 2 and exit at 3.

    c. Enter at 3 and exit at 4.

    d. Curve the thread to puff up the fabric slightly. Enter at 3 and exit at 5.

    e. Curve the thread again, enter at 2 and exit at 6.

    f. Reenter at 2 and exit at 6. Pinch up a ridge to form the eyebrow.

    g. Curve the thread around the ridge, enter at 7, and exit at 3.

    h. Pull the thread and enter at 3 and exit at 8.

    i. Pinch up a ridge to form the eyebrow. Curve the thread around the ridge, enter at 9, and exit at 2.

    j. Enter at 2 and exit at 10.

    k. Enter at 11 and exit at 12.

    l. Enter at 11 and pull the thread. Enter at 11 and exit at 2.

    m. Enter at 11 and exit at 2. Pull the thread tightly and lock the stitch.

    n. Enter at 2 and exit at 1, lock the stitch and cut the thread.

4. Wrap the gathered hose ends with Scotch tape to form a stem, cutting away any excess.

Figure H

Figure I

5. Spray the completed pumpkin with orange spray paint. Allow the paint to dry overnight.

6. Draw a triangle around the eyes and highlight the mouth using a black marker **(Figure H).**

7. Glue black buttons inside the eye triangles.

8. Cut a small rectangle of brown felt. Wrap and glue it over the Scotch tape on the stem.

9. A full-size leaf pattern is given in Figure F. Trace the pattern and cut 2 leaves from the green felt.

10. Glue the 2 leaves to each side of the stem.

Sectioning the pumpkin head

1. Use a needle and heavy-duty clear nylon thread to section the pumpkin head **(Figure I).**

    a. Insert the needle at the center bottom of the head.

    b. Pull the thread up the outside and enter at the top of the head next to the stem. Lock the stitch to hold it in place.

    c. Pull the thread down the opposite side of the head and enter at the center bottom. Lock the stitch.

2. Repeat steps a, b, and c three more times to complete the sectioning. When sectioning the face, enter the needle and thread underneath the nose and eyebrow ridges.

Bridal Shower Centerpiece

A lovely and very special addition to the party table that you can make yourself with hose and fabric scraps. Change the colors of the hair and flowers to match your own bride's hair and wedding colors.

Materials

1 pair of nude pantyhose.
½ yard of white cotton fabric.
Small amount of brown fiber.
1 yard of 1-inch-wide white eyelet trim.
2 small clusters of silk flowers; one white and one light blue.
1 yard of 3-inch-wide border lace.
2-foot length of white package yarn.
Heavy-duty white thread and a long sharp needle.
1 yard of light blue narrow satin ribbon.
Black and red narrow felt-tip markers.
Paper and pencil to enlarge the patterns.
Glue, scissors, white sewing thread, and straight pins.
½ pound of polyester fiberfill.
Powdered cheek blusher and 1 yard of net.

Making the sleeves and arms

1. Enlarge the patterns given in **Figure A** to full size. Cut 1 Dress Bottom, 2 Dress and 2 Sleeve pieces from white cotton fabric.

2. Turn the bottom edge of the Sleeve to the wrong side and stitch a ¼-inch hem. Topstitch eyelet trim over the hemmed edge **(Figure B)**. Fold the Sleeve right sides together and stitch the side seam.

3. Repeat step 2 for the remaining Sleeve.

4. Cut the toe portion from a pantyhose leg 9 inches from the bottom. Cut the same toe portion in half lengthwise **(Figure C)**. Sew each halve together along the bottom and sides to form 2 narrow tubes.

5. Turn the tubes right side out and stuff lightly to shape the arms. Each arm should be ½ inch in diameter and 1 inch longer than the sleeve.

6. Insert the arms inside the sleeves. Pin the sleeves to the side seams on 1 Dress piece at the shoulder line **(Figure D)**. Place the remaining Dress piece on top of the pinned sleeves, with the right side facing the sleeves.

7. Stitch the side seams, making sure that you stitch through all layers (including sleeves and arms). Leave the shoulder seams open and unstitched.

8. Pin the Dress Bottom to the lower edge of the dress, easing the dress to fit. Be sure to place right sides together **(Figure E)**. Stitch the seam ¼ inch from the edge.

9. Turn the assembled dress right side out, and stuff it firmly with polyester fiberfill.

10. Turn over a ⅛-inch hem along the unstitched shoulder seam and whipstitch the folded hems together.

Figure A

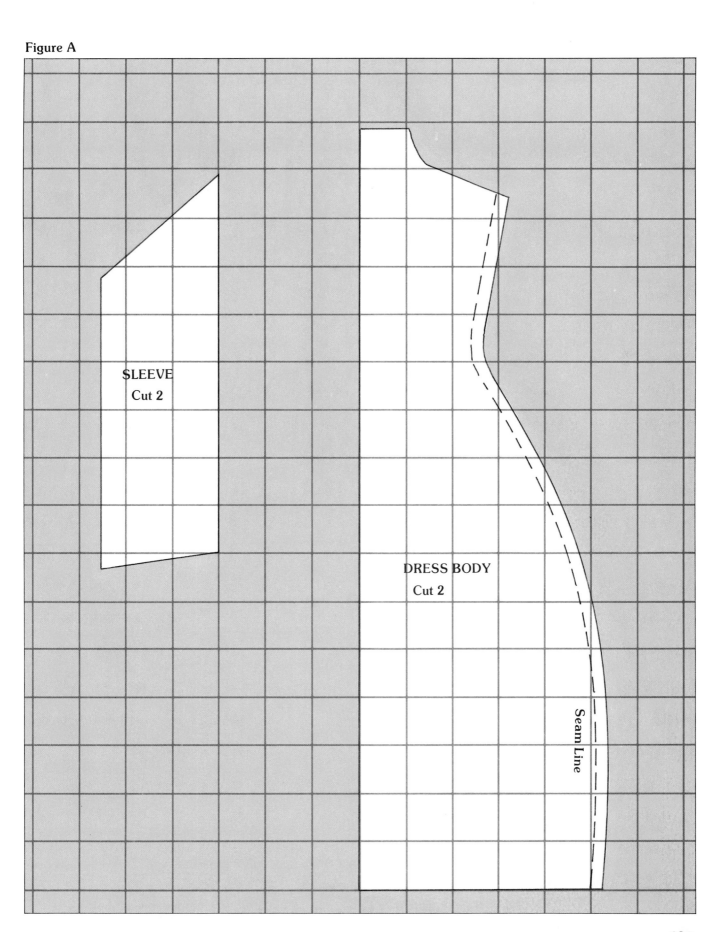

SLEEVE
Cut 2

DRESS BODY
Cut 2

Seam Line

Figure B

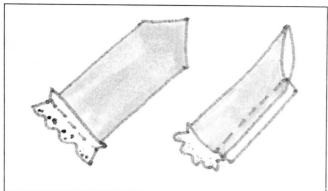

Figure C   **Figure D**

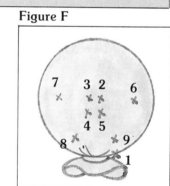

Figure E   **Figure F**

Making the head

1. Cut a 6-inch-diameter circle of pantyhose. Wrap the circle around a 4-inch-diameter ball of polyester fiberfill. Gather the raw edges of the hose at the bottom of the head and tie them together with thread.

2. Follow the illustrations given in **Figure F** to form the facial features. Use heavy-duty thread and a long sharp needle.

  a. Enter at 1 and exit at 2. Sew a circle of basting stitches approximately ½ inch in diameter, exiting at 3.

  b. Use the tip of the needle to very carefully lift the fiberfill within the circle just enough to make a small bulge. Gently pull the thread until a small round nose appears.

  c. Hold the thread with 1 hand and lock the stitch under the bridge of the nose, exiting at 2.

  d. To form the nostrils, reenter at 2 and exit at 4.

  e. Reenter slightly above 4 and exit at 3.

  f. Reenter at 3 and exit at 5.

  g. Reenter slightly above 5 and exit at 2. Lock the stitch under the bridge of the nose.

  h. To form the eyes, enter at 2 and exit at 6.

  i. Pull the thread over the surface, enter at 2 and exit at 3.

  j. Reenter at 3 and exit at 7.

  k. Pull the thread across the surface, enter at 3 and exit at 2. Gently pull the thread until the eyelid appears, and lock the stitch.

  l. To form the mouth, enter at 2 and exit at 8.

  m. Pull the thread across the surface, enter at 9 and exit at 3. Pull the thread until a smile appears.

  n. Reenter at 3 and exit at 1. Lock the stitch and cut the thread.

3. Draw the lips with a red marker and brush powdered cheek blusher on the cheeks.

4. Draw eyebrows and eyelashes with a black marker.

5. Cut 12-inch lengths of brown fiber. Stitch the center of each length to the head at the center part. Wrap the ends of the fiber lengths around each side of the head, and pull them up to the top of the head in the back. Twist and glue the ends of the fiber into a high bun.

Adding the lace trim and veil

1. Glue or stitch 3-inch-wide flat lace down the front of the dress. Begin the lace under the neck and end at the bottom seam of the dress, folding the raw ends to the underside. Wrap the remaining lace around the waist and tie a large bow in the back.

2. Glue or stitch eyelet trim around the shoulders.

3. Tie the narrow blue ribbon in a bow around the blue silk flowers. Tack the 2 hands together in the front to hold the bouquet.

4. Fold the yard of net in half. Gather the fold in your hands and tie the yarn tightly around the gathered fold.

5. Insert the white flowers inside the gathers. Place the gathered veil on the head with the flowers at the front and tie the yarn around the bun to hold it in place.

6. Pull half of the veil over the front of the completed doll.

Christi Christmas Witch

Hi! I'm Christi Christmas Witch! If you'll put me near your stocking, I'll tell Santa how good you were this year!

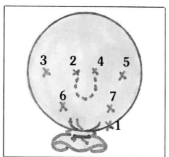

Figure A

Materials

2½-inch section cut from a cardboard paper towel roll.
⅛ yard of green and red small print fabric.
10½-inch length of pre-gathered lace trim.
8½-inch square of yellow felt.
Handful of polyester fiberfill.
2 black beads.
¼-inch-diameter wooden dowel rod, 4 inches long.
Toe portion cut from a pantyhose foot.
Small folding note card (the kind used for a Christmas package).
Sprig of artificial holly.
Scraps of red yarn.
Long sharp needle, heavy-duty thread, scissors, glue, 1 cotton swab, iron, ironing board, powdered cheek blusher, and a pen.
Paper and pencil for enlarging the patterns.

Making the head

1. Stretch the hose over a 4-inch ball of fiberfill to form the head. Tie the hose in a knot at the bottom and trim the excess with scissors.

2. Follow the entry and exit points shown in **Figure A** to form the face. Use a long needle and strong thread.

    a. Enter needle at 1 and exit at 2.

    b. Reenter at 2 and exit at 3.

    c. Pull the thread across the surface. Enter at 2 and exit at 4.

    d. Pull the thread across the surface. Enter at 5 and exit at 2. Pull the thread to form the eyes. Hold the thread tightly and lock the stitch.

    e. Raise the cheeks by gently lifting the fiberfill underneath the hose with the tip of the needle.

    f. Pinch the nose into a vertical ridge. Pull the thread around the bottom of the ridge. Enter at 4 and exit at 2. Hold the thread and lock the stitch.

    g. Use the tip of the needle to pull the cheeks out slightly.

    h. Reenter at 2 and exit at 6.

    i. Pull the thread across the surface. Enter at 7 and exit at 2. Pull the thread tightly to form the mouth. Hold the thread and lock the stitch.

    j. Use the tip of the needle to pull the chin out slightly.

Figure B

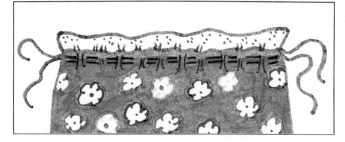

Figure C

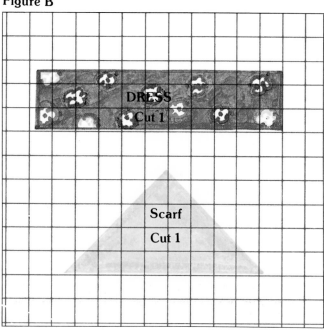

Figure D

3. Glue black beads into the eye indentations.

4. Use a cotton swab to brush powdered blusher on the cheeks.

5. Glue the completed head to the top of the cardboard tube, hiding the tied portion inside.

6. Glue a tuft of fiberfill to the top of the head at the front hairline.

Making the dress

1. Enlarge the pattern pieces given in **Figure B** to full size.

2. Cut the dress from green and red print fabric using the full-size pattern.

3. Sew a ¼-inch hem on the two long edges of the dress piece.

4. Topstitch the lace trim over one hemmed edge.

5. Gather the dress ¼ inch below the lace **(Figure C).** Wrap the gathered dress around the cardboard tube, placing the lace edge next to the face.

6. Pull the gathering threads to fit the neckline and tie them in a knot at the back. Glue the dress to the cardboard tube around the neckline.

7. Wrap a length of yarn around the neck gathers and tie a bow in front.

Finishing

1. Cut the scarf from yellow felt using the full-size pattern.

2. Wrap the long edge of the felt triangle around the face. Stitch the ends of the triangle together at the back of the neck **(Figure D).** Stitch the back of the triangle to the back of the head.

3. Glue the sprig of artificial holly to one end of a dowel. Slip the dowel under the yarn tied around the neck.

4. Write a note on the folding note card that says: "Hi! I'm Christi Christmas Witch. Put me near your stocking and I'll tell Santa how good you were this year!"

5. Tie the note to the wooden dowel with a piece of yarn.

Santa & Mrs. Claus

This cheerful Christmas couple will brighten your holiday home. Place them on your mantel, underneath your tree, or on a chair in your entry hall. They will carefully hold presents, cards, or just help with the fun.

Materials

For each body you will need the following:
8- or 9-inch diameter clay flowerpot.
1 pair of sandal-toe pantyhose.
1 pound of polyester fiberfill.
1 skein of white rug yarn.
Red and blue embroidery thread.
String, glue, pliers, straight pins, sewing thread (to match the fabrics), iron and ironing board, and heavy-duty brown sewing thread.
Pencil and paper to enlarge the patterns.

To make Mrs. Santa's clothes you will need:
    1½ yards of red cotton fabric.
    ½ yard of red and white polka-dot fabric.
    1 pair of white baby socks.
    1 pair of white baby shoes.
    1 package of white rick-rack.
    2 yards of ½-inch-wide white eyelet trim.
    1 coat hanger.
    1 sheet of clear acetate (the kind used for covering pictures in albums).
    Instant-bonding glue.
    2 wooden shiskebob skewers and a small ball of yarn.

To make Santa's clothes you need:
    4-inch-square piece of gold felt.
    32 x 2¼-inch piece of black felt.
    2½ yards of red cotton fabric.
    14 x 28-inch piece of natural muslin fabric.
    1 pair of black high-topped baby shoes.
    1 pair of black wool baby mittens.
    ½ yard of wide green ribbon.
    Black laundry marker and carbon paper.

Figure A

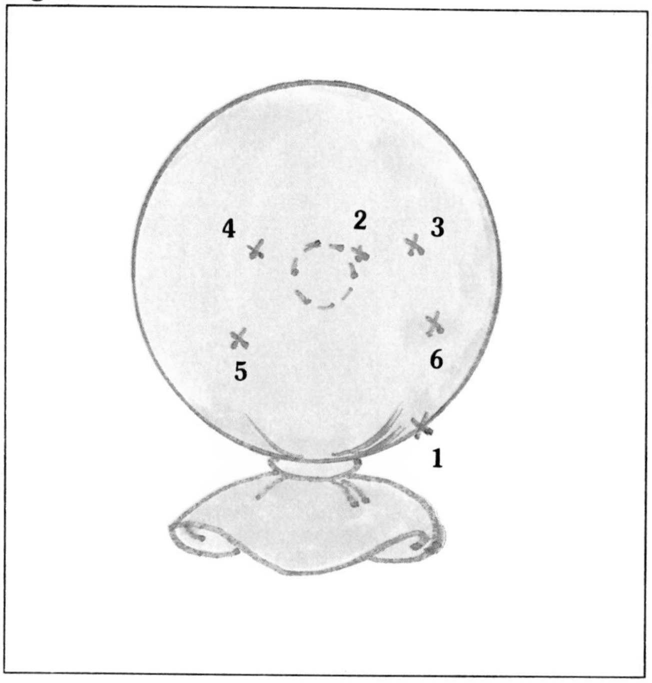

Figure B

Figure C

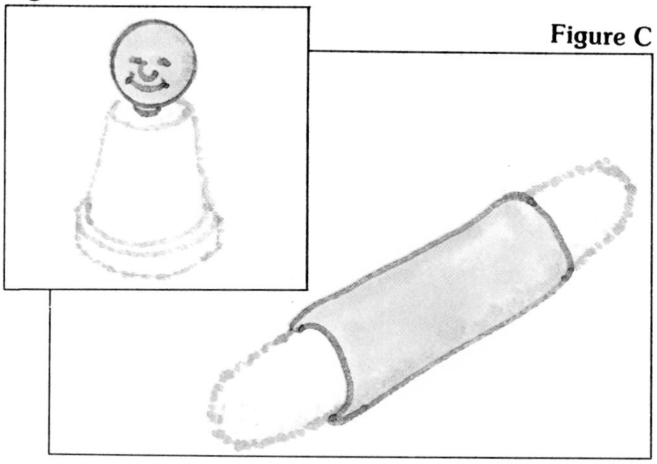

Figure D

Figure E

Making the head

1. Cut the foot from a pair of pantyhose about 2 inches above the ankle.

2. Form a smooth ball of fiberfill, about 19 inches in circumference. Compress and stuff the fiberfill into the hose foot to form a round "head" about 13 inches in circumference.

3. Pull part of the fiberfill down into the "neck" to prevent it from wobbling. Wrap string securely around the "neck" and tie it in a knot.

4. To form the facial features, thread a needle with heavy-duty thread and follow the illustrations in **Figure A.**

    a. Enter the needle at 1 and exit on the face area at 2.
    b. Pinch up a round "button" of fiberfill to suggest a nose and work small gathering stitches around the button, ending at 2.
    c. Pull the thread to form the nose and lock the stitch.
    d. Reenter at 2 and exit at 1. Lock the stitch.
    e. To form the eyes, reenter at 1 and exit at 3. Reenter at 3 and exit at 1. Lock the stitch. Repeat for the other eye at point 4.
    f. To form the mouth, make 2 "dimples" in the same manner as the eyes, at points 5 and 6.

5. On Mrs. Claus only, connect the 2 "dimples" using a full strand of red embroidery floss and the split stitch. Illustrated instructions for embroidery stitches are given in the "Tips and Techniques" section at the beginning of this book.

6. Embroider the eye sockets with the satin stitch using a full strand of embroidery floss. Use blue for Mrs. Claus and brown for Santa.

Making the body

1. Invert the flower pot and wrap it with a thin layer of fiberfill. Attach the head by pulling the "neck" through the hole in the bottom of the flower pot. The neck should fit very tightly inside the hole **(Figure B).**

2. Cut a 20-inch length of hose for the legs. Form a 30-inch cylinder of fiberfill about 2 inches in diameter. Pull the 20-inch length of hose over the 30-inch cylinder **(Figure C).** Pull the ends of the hose until it is stretched to the length of the cylinder. Tie string around each end of the cylinder. This cylinder will form both legs.

3. Cut a long piece of string. Tie the middle of the string securely around the center of the leg cylinder. Tie a knot.

4. Place the legs at the front of the flower pot. Wrap the long ends of the string completely around the flower pot, using the lip of the pot as a guideline. Tie the string in a knot **(Figure D).**

5. Cut a 20-inch length of hose for the arms. This length should include the toe portion of the hose. Form a 30-inch cylinder of fiberfill.

6. Pull the 20-inch length of hose over the 30-inch cylinder as you did for the legs. Stretch the hose to the length of the cylinder.

7. Turn the raw edges on the open end of the hose to the inside. Hand stitch the folded edges together.

8. Place the center of the arm cylinder at the back of the neck, forcing it between the head and the flowerpot as shown in **Figure E.**

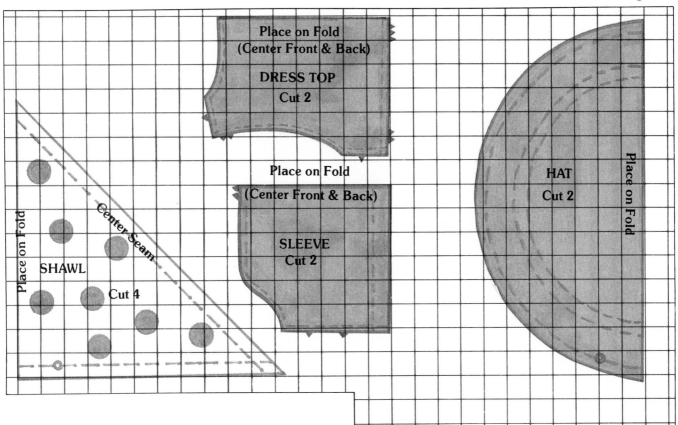

Place on Fold
(Center Front & Back)

DRESS TOP

Cut 2

Place on Fold
(Center Front & Back)

SLEEVE
Cut 2

Place on Fold

SHAWL

Cut 4

Center Seam

HAT
Cut 2

Place on Fold

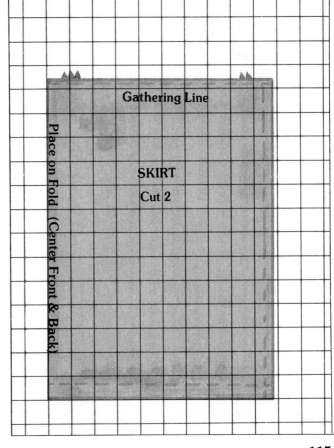

Gathering Line

Place on Fold (Center Front & Back)

SKIRT

Cut 2

Mrs. Santa's clothes

1. Enlarge the patterns shown in **Figure F** to full size. Cut each of the pattern pieces from the appropriate color of fabric.

2. Place the 2 Dress Tops right sides together and sew the shoulder seams.

3. Slit the center back about 6 inches deep **(Figure G)**. Turn the raw edges under along the slit and around the neck opening. Topstitch.

4. Gather the top of one Sleeve and pin it to the open armhole, placing right sides together. Ease the gathers to fit and stitch the pinned seam **(Figure H)**.

5. Hem the lower edge of the sleeves, turning the raw edges to the wrong side. Topstitch rick-rack over the hem.

6. Sew the underarm and side seams **(Figure I)**.

7. Sew the 2 Skirt pieces right sides together at the side seams.

8. Turn up the hem allowance on the skirt and stitch. Stitch rick-rack around the bottom of the skirt.

9. Gather the top of the skirt along the gathering line.

10. With right sides together, sew the skirt to the dress top, matching notches and easing the gathers to fit.

11. Slip the dress over the body and hand tack the neck opening closed in the back.

Figure G

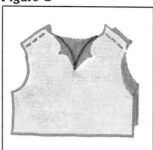

Figure H

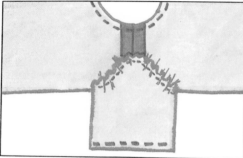

Figure I

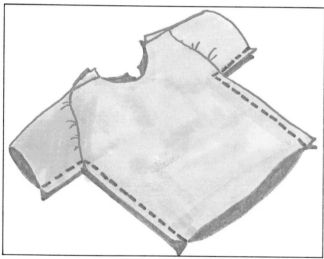

Figure J

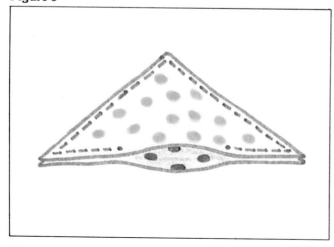

Figure K

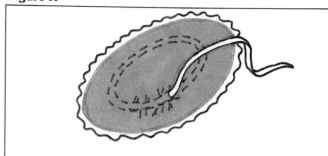

Figure L

Shawl, bonnet, glasses, and knitting

1. Pin the 2 Shawl pieces right sides together and sew around all 3 sides, leaving an opening between the small circles (**Figure J**).

2. Clip the corners and turn the shawl right side out. Turn the remaining raw edges to the inside and press the shawl.

3. Topstitch along the longest side. Topstitch eyelet trim along the 2 short sides.

4. Stitch the 2 Bonnet pieces right sides together, leaving an opening between the 2 small circles. Clip the seams and turn the bonnet right side out. Turn the remaining raw edges to the inside and press. Topstitch rick-rack around the edges.

5. Topstitch each of the bonnet casing lines. Cut a small slit between the 2 casing lines (through 1 layer of the hat) as shown in **Figure K.** Insert the elastic through the casing.

6. Pull the ends of the elastic to gather the bonnet. Place the bonnet on the head and adjust the gathers until it fits. Securely sew the ends of the elastic together. Cut off the excess, and pull the elastic back inside the casing. Whipstitch the slit in the casing closed.

7. Use a pair of pliers to bend the coat hanger into glasses as shown in **Figure L**.

8. Cut 2 semi-circles of clear acetate and glue them to the coat hanger glasses with instant-bonding glue.

9. Knit several rows with yarn using the shiskebob skewers as knitting needles. Place the "needles" in Mrs. Claus' hand and tack the ball of yarn to her skirt.

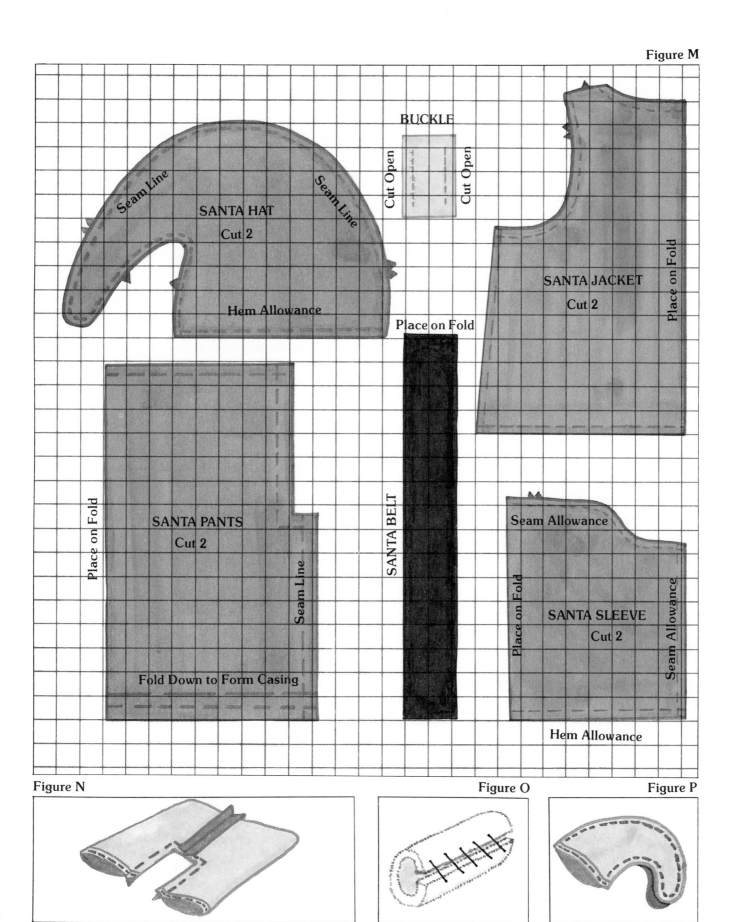

BUCKLE

Cut Open

Cut Open

Seam Line

Seam Line

SANTA HAT

Cut 2

Hem Allowance

Place on Fold

SANTA JACKET

Cut 2

Place on Fold

Place on Fold

SANTA PANTS

Cut 2

Seam Line

SANTA BELT

Seam Allowance

Place on Fold

SANTA SLEEVE

Cut 2

Seam Allowance

Fold Down to Form Casing

Hem Allowance

Figure N

Figure O

Figure P

117

Figure Q

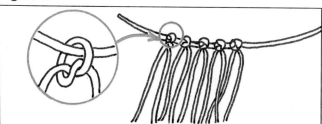

Figure R

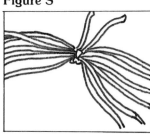

Figure S

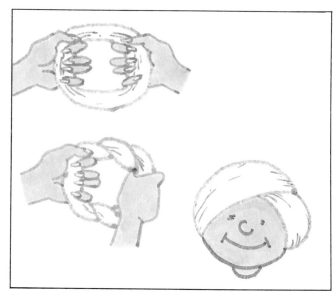

Figure T

Santa's clothes

1. Enlarge the patterns shown in **Figure M** to full size. Cut each of them from the appropriate color of fabric.

2. Make Santa's jacket in the same manner as Mrs. Santa's dress top, following steps 2 through 6, but omitting the rickrack trim.

3. Sew the Pants right sides together along the center seams. Sew a ½-inch hem in the pant bottom.

4. Refold the pants so the seams are at the center front and back (**Figure N**). Sew the inside leg seams.

5. Turn the casing allowance to the wrong side and stitch.

6. Cut a small slit on the inside of the casing. Cut a 36-inch length of string. Thread the string through the casing and pull the ends to gather the waist.

7. Turn the pants right side out. Slip the pants over the legs and the rim of the flower pot. Pull the casing string tightly around the rim and tie it to hold the pants in place.

8. Slip the jacket over the head and tack the neck openings closed in the back.

9. Cut lengths of bonded fiberfill in 5-inch widths. Fold the long edges on each length together and whipstitch them (**Figure O**). Trim the sleeves, legs, and jacket with the whip-stitched lengths, cutting them to fit. Place the whipstitched side toward the clothing when you stitch them to the fabric.

Hat, belt, and "goodies" bag

1. Sew the 2 Hat pieces right sides together. Turn up and sew a ¼-inch hem around the bottom of the hat (**Figure P**).

2. Clip the seam allowance and turn the hat right side out.

3. Use rug yarn to make the hat tassel. Wind a generous amount of rug yarn around 4 fingers. Remove the yarn from your fingers, and tie a short piece of yarn around the center of the loops. Cut the loop ends and sew the finished tassel on the end of the hat.

4. Trim the bottom of the hat with fiberfill in the same manner as you did for the other clothing.

5. Cut open the slits in the Buckle. Wrap the black felt belt around Santa's waist. Thread one end of the belt up through the buckle slit and down through the other slit. Tack the belt in place.

6. Fold the muslin fabric in half to form a 14-inch square for Santa's "goodies" bag. Sew both sides seams (**Figure Q**).

7. Turn the top hem allowance to the wrong side and stitch. Turn the bag right side out.

8. Transfer the enlarged "goodies" design to the front of the bag using carbon paper and a soft pencil. Color the letters on the bag with a laundry marker.

9. Stuff the bag with newspapers or rags and add a small toy at the top. Tie the top together with a wide green ribbon.

Finishing

1. To make Santa's beard, cut a 12-inch length of rug yarn to use as a holding cord. Cut additional 12-inch lengths of yarn and tie each of them individually over the holding cord with the knot in the middle. Continue the cut and tie yarn lengths until the beard is full (**Figure R**).

2. Sew the completed beard to Santa's chin. Trim the ends evenly with scissors.

3. To form Santa's moustache, cut several 6-inch lengths of rug yarn. Tie the yarn lengths in the center (**Figure S**).

4. Sew the moustache to Santa's face above the mouth. Trim the ends with scissors.

5. To make Mrs. Santa's hair, use a full skein of rug yarn. Remove the label carefully, and you should find that the rug yarn is coiled in a single circular roll. Grip and hold the roll with your left hand, and twist the opposite side of the roll about 3 times with your right hand (**Figure T**).

6. Set the roll on top of Mrs. Santa's head and tack it in place with sewing thread.

7. Place Mrs. Santa's bonnet on top of the hair and tack it in place.

Easter Table Centerpiece

This easy-to-make table decoration will brighten Easter for parents and children alike. The same bunny can be tucked inside a child's Easter basket.

Materials

1 leg of nurse's white pantyhose.
½ pound of polyester fiberfill.
4 x 6-inch piece of white felt.
4 x 6-inch piece of cardboard.
2 small black beads.
2-inch square of pink felt.
½ yard of ½-inch-wide green grosgrain ribbon.
Sprig of tiny artificial flowers.
1 yard of pastel plaid ribbon.
10 or 12 pantyhose egg containers in pastel colors.
Easter basket and straw.
Pink waterproof marker, sewing needle, heavy-duty white thread, scissors, powdered cheek blusher. and straight pins.

Body and ears

1. Cut the foot from a pantyhose leg 8 inches above the ankle. Turn the hose wrong side out.

Figure A

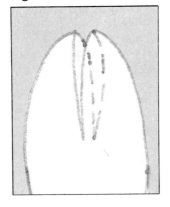

Figure B

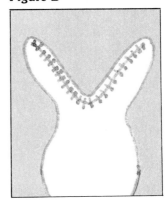

2. Cut a 4-inch-long slit down the center of the toe to form the ears **(Figure A)**. Pull the 2 "ears" out and trim the raw edges into a gentle curve **(Figure B)**. Stitch ¼ inch from the raw edges.

119

Figure E

Figure C

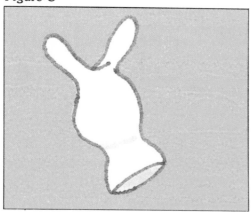

Figure F

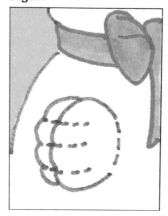

Figure G

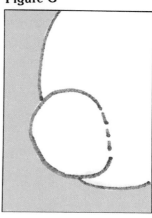

Figure D

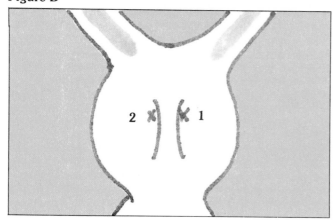

3. Turn the hose right side out and stuff the ears lightly. Continue to stuff the hose below the ears to form a well-rounded head **(Figure C).**

4. Stuff the remainder of the hose to form a body. Tie the hose in a knot at the bottom of the body.

5. Wipe powdered cheek blusher on the center front of both ears.

Face

1. Pinch up a vertical ridge in the center of the face. Use heavy-duty white thread and follow the illustrations in **Figure D** to form the facial features.

    a. Enter at 1 and exit at 2. Return to 1 and pull the thread to tighten.

    b. Pull the thread around the bottom of the ridge; enter at 2 and exit at 1.

    c. Pull the thread over the ridge; enter at 2 and exit at 1.

    d. To form the mouth, reenter at 1, and exit 1 inch below the nose. Enter the needle just under the nose and exit at 2. Pull the thread firmly and lock the stitch in the eye indentation.

2. Glue black beads in each eye indentation.

3. Cut 2 pink felt eyelashes using the full size pattern **(Figure H)** and glue 1 on the outside of each eye bead.

4. Color the lower half of the nose and outline the mouth using a pink marker.

5. Tie the green grosgrain bow tightly around the neck to separate the head from the body.

120

Paws and tail

1. Sew a circle of basting stitches about 1½ inches in diameter just below the tied ribbon bow. Pull the thread tightly to form a ball. Take a vertical stitch across the center on the surface of the ball to divide it into 2 equal parts **(Figure E)**.

2. Take 3 evenly-spaced small stitches on each side of the dividing line and pull the thread to form little fingers as shown in **Figure F.** Lock the stitch below the paws.

3. Brush the knuckles with powdered cheek blusher.

4. To form the tail, sew a circle of basting stitches about 1¼ inches in diameter at the lower back of the body. Pull the thread to form a ball, and lock the stitches **(Figure G)**.

Feet

1. Cut 2 Foot pieces, one from cardboard and one from white felt, using the full-size pattern given in Figure H.

2. Glue the felt and cardboard Foot pieces together.

3. Center the body over the feet and glue them together.

4. Draw the lines for the toes using a pink marker. Refer to Figure H for placement.

5. Slip the tiny flowers through the ribbon bow at the neck.

Finishing

1. Place a layer of straw inside an Easter basket.

2. Place the completed bunny on one side of the basket and surround him with pastel-colored egg containers.

3. Tie a pastel plaid bow and attach it to one side of the finished basket.

Figure H

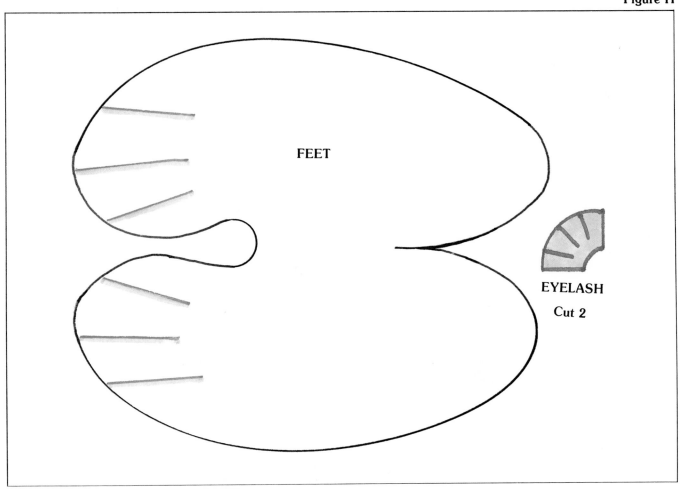

FEET

EYELASH

Cut 2

Christmas Ornaments

Perky Christmas ornaments to brighten your home this year. Hang them on the tree, decorate packages or wreaths, or give them as special Christmas gifts.

Materials

To make the Santa ornament:
    8-inch square piece of red felt.
    1 leg cut from a pair of pantyhose.
    Sprig of artificial holly.
    Small amount of polyester fiberfill.
    7-inch length of gold elastic.
    Red and black felt-tip markers.

To make the reindeer ornament:
    1 leg cut from a pair of brown heavy "winter" pantyhose.
    Small amount of polyester fiberfill.
    2 small white buttons with a smooth top and a bottom shank.
    ¼ yard of green calico fabric.
    7-inch length of gold elastic.
    Sprig of artificial holly.
    4-inch square piece of brown felt.
    6-inch square piece of heavy cardboard.
    Red pompom.
    Black felt-tip marker.

To make the baby angel ornament:
    6-inch square piece of white felt.
    16-inch length of 3½-inch-wide flat lace.
    1 leg cut from a pair of nurse's white pantyhose.
    Small amount of polyester fiberfill.
    Small amount of yellow fiber.
    1 silver pipe cleaner.
    10-inch length of white yarn.
Heavy-duty clear nylon thread and a long sharp needle.
Glue, scissors, pencil, and tracing paper.

Making the Santa ornament
The head

1. Cut a 6-inch-diameter circle of pantyhose. Wrap the circle around a 4-inch-diameter ball of polyester fiberfill. Gather the raw edges of the hose at the bottom of the head and tie them together with thread.

2. Use a long sharp needle and heavy-duty thread to form the nose. Follow the entry and exit points illustrated in **Figure A.**

    a. Enter at 1 and exit at 2. Sew a circle of basting stitches approximately ½ inch in diameter, exiting at 3.

    b. Use the tip of the needle to carefully lift the fiberfill within the circle just enough to make a small bulge. Gently pull the thread until a nice round nose appears.

    c. Hold the thread with 1 hand and lock the stitch under the bridge of the nose, exiting at 2.

    d. To form the nostrils, reenter at 2 and exit at 4.

    e. Reenter ¼ inch above 4 and exit at 3.

    f. Reenter at 3 and exit at 5.

    g. Reenter ¼ inch above 5 and exit at 2. Lock the stitch under the bridge of the nose.

3. To form the eyes and mouth, again follow the entry and exit points given in Figure A.

    a. To begin the mouth, enter at 2 and exit at 8.

    b. Pull the thread across the surface, enter at 9 and exit at 3. Pull the thread until a smile appears.

    c. Reenter at 3 and exit at 1.

    d. Lock the stitch and cut the thread.

    e. To form the eyes, enter at 1 and exit at 2.

    f. Reenter at 2 and exit at 6.

    g. Pull the thread over the surface, enter at 2 and exit at 3.

    h. Reenter at 3 and exit at 7.

    i. Pull the thread across the surface, enter at 3 and exit at 2. Gently pull the thread until the closed eyes appear. Lock the stitch.

    j. Reenter at 2 and exit at 1. Lock the stitch and cut the thread.

4. Draw lips on the mouth line with a red felt-tip marker. Draw a line over the eye lines with a black felt-tip marker.

Figure A

Figure B

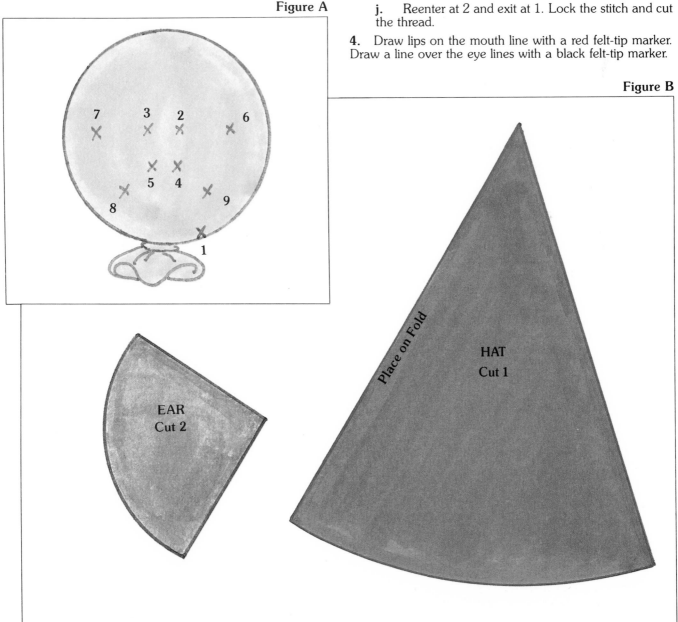

EAR
Cut 2

Place on Fold

HAT
Cut 1

Figure B

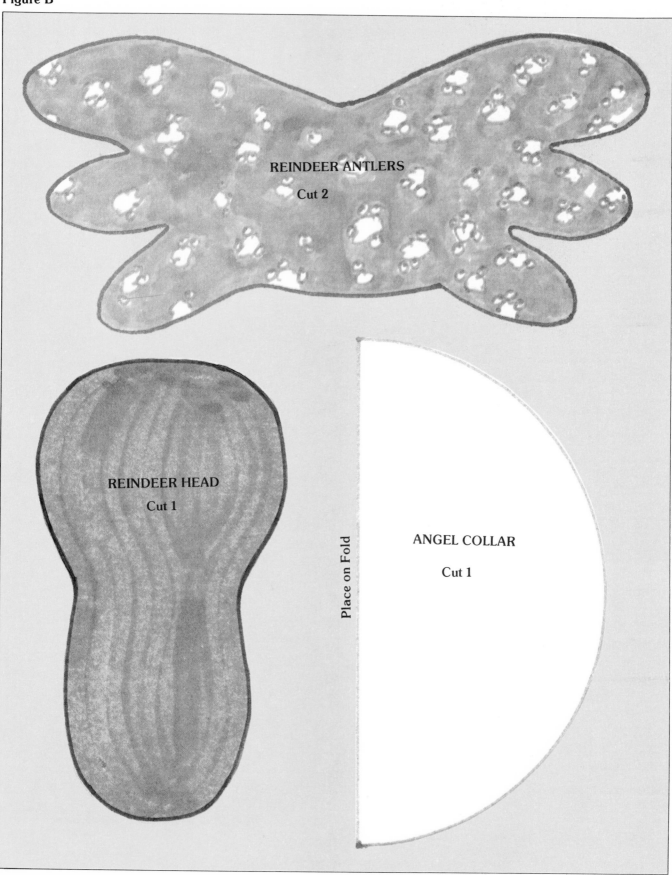

REINDEER ANTLERS

Cut 2

REINDEER HEAD

Cut 1

Place on Fold

ANGEL COLLAR

Cut 1

The hat

1. The full-size pattern for Santa's hat is given in **Figure B.** Trace the full-size pattern and cut the hat piece from red felt, following the "place on fold" notations given.

2. Fold the Hat piece right sides together and stitch along the back seam allowance.

3. Turn the hat right side out and glue it to the top of the pantyhose head.

4. Form a small amount of polyester fiberfill into a ball and glue it to the tip of the hat.

5. Glue a ½-inch-wide band of polyester fiberfill around the lower edge of the hat. Fold the tip of the hat to one side **(Figure C).**

6. Tie a knot in the ends of the gold elastic to form a hanging loop. Hand tack the loop to the fold in the hat.

Finishing

1. Glue a layer of polyester fiberfill completely around the lower portion of the head to form the beard. Leave the mouth uncovered.

2. Twist a small amount of fiberfill to form a moustache, and glue it beneath the nose.

3. Hand tack the sprig of artificial holly to the side of the hat **(Figure D).**

Making the reindeer ornament
The head

1. Cut the toe from a pair of brown heavy "winter" pantyhose, 7 inches above the bottom seam.

2. Full-size patterns for the reindeer's antlers, head, and ears are given in Figure B. Trace the patterns using tracing paper and a pencil. Transfer the head pattern to heavy cardboard, and cut it out.

3. Glue polyester fiberfill around the edges of the cardboard head **(Figure E).**

4. Insert the cardboard head inside the toe of the hose.

5. Generously stuff the hose with fiberfill above and below the cardboard.

6. Gather the opening in the hose at the back of the head using a needle and heavy-duty thread. Pull the gathering thread to close the opening and lock the stitch.

7. Cut 2 Antlers from green calico fabric using the full-size pattern. Place the 2 Antlers right sides together, and stitch around the seam allowance. Leave an unstitched opening large enough to turn and stuff the antlers **(Figure F).**

8. Turn the antlers right side out and stuff them lightly. Whipstitch the opening closed.

9. Whipstitch the completed antlers to the back of the head **(Figure G).**

Figure C

Figure D

Figure E

Figure F

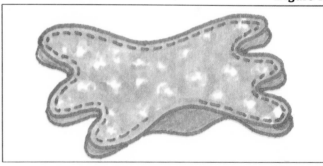

Figure G

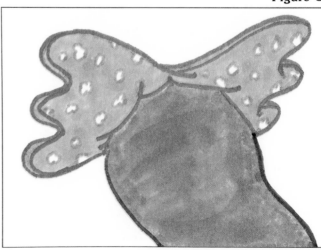

Figure H

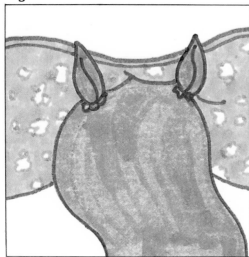

Finishing

1. Cut 2 Ears from brown felt.

2. Fold each ear in half placing the 2 straight sides together. Whipstitch the ears to either side of the head in front of the antlers **(Figure H)**.

3. Follow the illustrations given in **Figure I** to form the facial features.

> **a.** Pinch up a vertical ridge in the center of the head and take a deep stitch back and forth underneath the ridge to secure it. Lock the stitch.

> **b.** Pinch up an eyebrow ridge at an angle above each eye, and stitch back and forth underneath the ridge. Lock the stitch and cut the thread.

4. Use the black laundry marker to draw black pupils in the center of each white button. Glue the buttons into the eye indentations.

5. Glue the pompom to the end of the nose. Glue or stitch a sprig of artificial holly to the top of the head.

6. Tie a knot in the ends of the gold elastic to form a hanging loop. Hand tack the loop to the top of the head.

Figure I

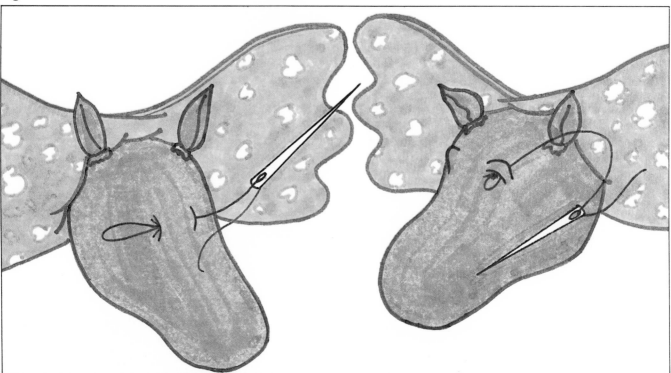

Making the baby angel ornament
The head

1. To make the baby angel head, use white hose and follow the instructions given in steps 1 through 3 under "Making the Santa ornament — The head."

2. A full-size pattern for the angel's collar is given in Figure B. Trace the collar pattern and cut it from white felt, placing the straight pattern edge on a fold.

3. Gather one edge of the flat lace using a needle and heavy-duty thread.

4. Pin the gathered lace to the felt collar 1½ inches from the edge, adjusting the gathers to fit evenly around the collar. Topstitch along the gathered edge of the lace **(Figure J).**

5. Position the head in the center of the collar. Whipstitch around the neck to secure the head to the collar. Fold the collar at the shoulder line **(Figure K).**

The hands

1. To make 1 hand, form a small ball of polyester fiberfill and wrap it with a 2-inch-diameter circle cut from white hose. Gather the raw edges of the hose at the bottom of the ball and tie them together with thread.

2. Take a vertical stitch across the center front of the ball to divide it into 2 equal parts **(Figure L).**

3. Take 3 evenly spaced small stitches on each side of the dividing line and pull the thread to form little fingers as shown in **Figure M.**

4. Return the thread to the gathered area on the bottom and lock the stitch. Whipstitch the hands in place below the chin.

Finishing

1. Glue a tuft of yellow fiber to the top of the head for hair.

2. Shape a silver pipe cleaner into a 2-inch-diameter circle and glue it on top of the fiber hair.

3. Tie the ends of the white yarn together to form a hanging loop. Hand tack the loop to the back of the head.

Figure J

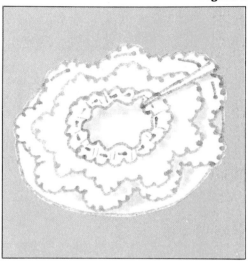

Figure K

Figure L

Figure M

Thanksgiving Turkey

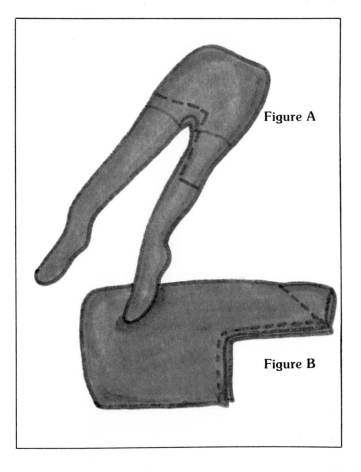

This delightful stuffed bird will be a decorative addition to your Thanksgiving table – or tuck a brick inside and use him as a unique doorstop.

Materials

1 pair each of heavy "winter" pantyhose in 4 different colors: brown, wine, gray, and navy blue.
2 small black beads.
12-inch square piece of yellow felt.
Heavy-duty thread and a long sharp needle.
1 pound of polyester fiberfill and a brick (if you plan to use the finished turkey for a doorstop).
Scissors and glue.
Pencil and paper to enlarge the pattern.

Making the body

1. Turn the pair of brown pantyhose wrong side out and place it on a flat surface. Cut the turkey body following the illustration given in **Figure A.**

2. To form the head stitch diagonally across the cut edge following the illustration in **Figure B.**

3. Turn the hose right side out. Stuff the head and neck with polyester fiberfill until they are slightly rounded. Stuff the body with fiberfill until it fills out **(Figure C)**. If you plan to use the finished turkey as a doorstop, wrap a brick with fiberfill and insert it in the center of the body.

4. Pull the head upright and adjust the fiberfill to form the throat. To hold the head upright, whipstitch the back of the neck to the body **(Figure D).**

Figure A

Figure B

Figure C

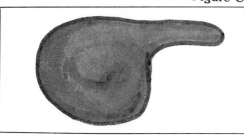

Figure D

Figure E

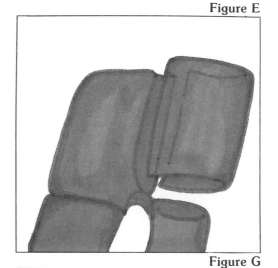

Figure F

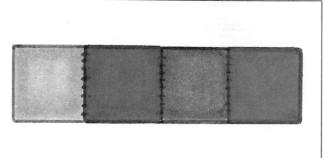

Figure G

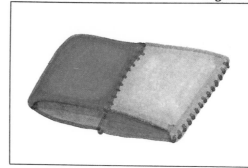

Figure H

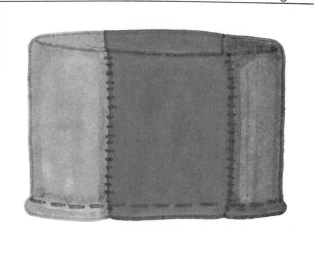

Tail

1. Cut 4 rectangles from the panty portion of the hose as illustrated in **Figure E.** Cut 2 rectangles from the wine hose and 1 rectangle each from the brown and gray hose.

2. Sew the long edges of the rectangles together to form a continuous panel, alternating the colors as illustrated in **Figure F.**

3. Stitch the ends of the panel right sides together to form a tube **(Figure G).**

4. Fold the tube in half, placing right sides together so the 2 wine panels are back to back.

5. Stitch through both layers of the folded tube ⅝ inch from the bottom edge **(Figure H).** Turn the stitched tube right side out.

6. Stuff the tube lightly to form the tail. Gather the opening with a needle and heavy-duty thread. Pull the gathering threads to close the opening and lock the stitch.

Figure K

Figure L

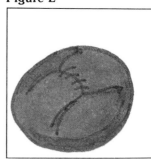

Figure M

Figure N

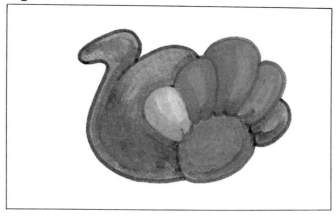

Figure I

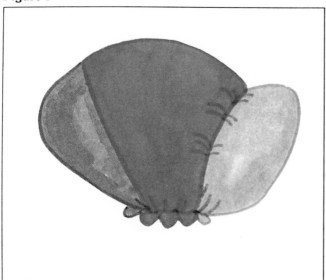

Figure J

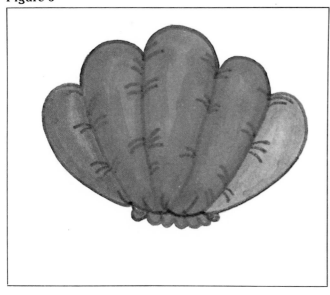

7. Rethread the needle with heavy-duty thread. Insert the needle at the gathered area. Wrap the thread completely around the tail over the seam line (between the wine and brown rectangles) returning to the gathered area **(Figure I)**. Pull the thread to tighten it and lock the stitch.

8. Repeat step 7 three more times, dividing the wine rectangles into 3 sections and separating the wine and gray rectangles along the seam line **(Figure J)**. Pull the thread and lock the stitch.

9. Cut a 6-inch section of blue hose, and stuff it lightly with polyester fiberfill **(Figure K)**.

10. Shape the stuffed tube into a flat circle, folding the raw edges of the hose to the back. Whipstitch the raw edges flat against the back **(Figure L)**.

11. Whipstitch the completed circle over the gathered area on the tail **(Figure M)**.

12. Whipstitch the assembled tail over the opening in the body, making sure to completely cover all raw edges **(Figure N)**.

130

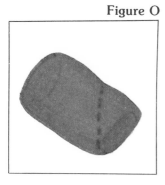

Figure O

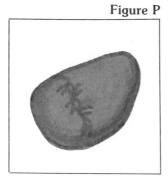

Figure P

Figure Q

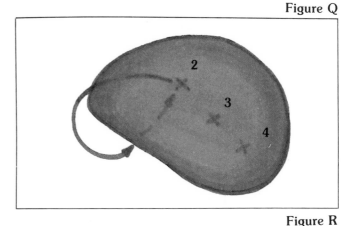

Wings

1. To make 1 wing, cut a section of wine hose 6 inches long. Stitch diagonally across one end of the section as shown in **Figure O.** Turn the hose right side out and stuff it lightly with fiberfill.

2. Fold the raw edges to the back of the wing and whipstitch them in place **(Figure P).**

3. Follow the entry and exit points given in **Figure Q** to complete the wings.

    a. Enter on the back side and exit at 2.

    b. Wrap the thread around the diagonal seam. Enter on the back of the wing behind 2 and exit at 2.

    c. Pull the thread to tighten and lock the stitch.

    d. Reenter at 2 and exit at 3.

    e. Repeat steps b, c, and d two more times (at points 3 and 4) to complete the wing.

4. Repeat steps 1 through 3 to make the other wing.

5. Whipstitch the wings to the sides of the body, placing the folded raw edges against the body.

Feet and beak

1. Enlarge the pattern given in **Figure R** to full size, and cut the feet from yellow felt.

2. Whipstitch the feet to the underside of the body.

3. Measure the size of the hose beak and cut a triangle of yellow felt to cover it.

4. Stitch or glue the triangle over the hose beak.

Eyes and wattle

1. Pinch up a deep ridge in the center of the head. Stitch back and forth underneath the ridge to form the eye indentations. Lock the stitch. Glue small black beads in the indentations.

2. Cut a 5-inch toe section from wine hose. Cut the section in half lengthwise **(Figure S).**

3. Stitch the cut edges together on each half and turn the resulting tubes right side out.

4. Turn the raw edges on the open end of the tubes to the inside. Whipstitch one tube to the top of the head, allowing it to trail to one side. Stitch the remaining tube just under the head along the front chest seam **(Figure T).**

Figure R

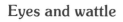

FEET

Cut 1

Figure S

Figure T

Christmas Treetop Angel

A lacy Victorian angel to top your Christmas tree for years to come.

Materials

1 leg of pantyhose.
Small amount of polyester fiberfill.
Small amount of white yarn.
12-inch square piece of white cotton fabric.
12-inch square piece of lace fabric.
1 yard of 5-inch-wide flat lace.
2-inch-diameter lacy flower.
1 yard of 1-inch-wide flat lace.
Liquid starch and glue.
Red and black felt-tip markers.
Scissors, straight pins and iron.
Powdered cheek blusher.
Cardboard tube from a paper towel roll.
Paper and pencil to enlarge the patterns.
Heavy-duty thread and a long sharp needle.

Making the body

1. Enlarge the patterns given in **Figure A** to full size. Cut 1 Gown piece from white cotton fabric. Pay particular attention to the "place on fold" notations.

2. Cut a 24-inch length of 5-inch-wide lace. Gather the lace 1 inch from the edge.

3. Pull the gathering threads and pin the lace along the bottom edge of the Gown, easing the gathers to fit **(Figure B)**. Topstitch the lace to the Gown, stitching over the gathering threads.

4. Fold the top of the gathered lace down toward the bottom of the gown and whipstitch it in place **(Figure C)**.

5. Cut a 12-inch length of 1-inch-wide flat lace and gather it along one edge.

6. Pull the gathering threads and pin the lace along the top edge of the gown, easing the gathers to fit **(Figure D)**. Topstitch along the gathering threads.

7. Cut a 4-inch section of cardboard tube. Wrap the top of the gown around 1 end of the cardboard tube and glue it in place **(Figure E)**.

8. Cut a 2-foot length of white yarn. Double it and wrap it around the neckline. Tie the yarn in a bow in front and trim the ends.

Figure A

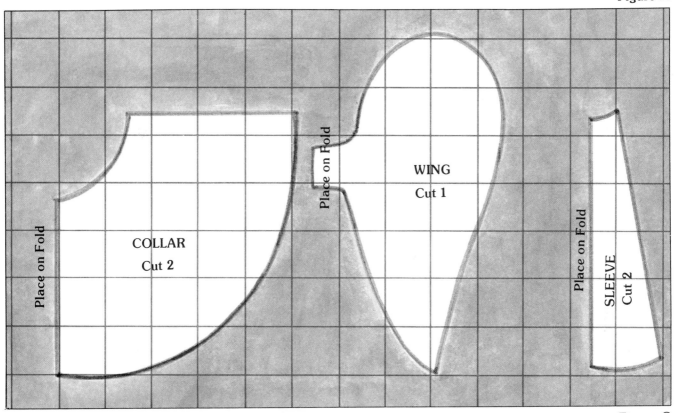

Place on Fold

COLLAR
Cut 2

Place on Fold

WING
Cut 1

Place on Fold

SLEEVE
Cut 2

Figure B

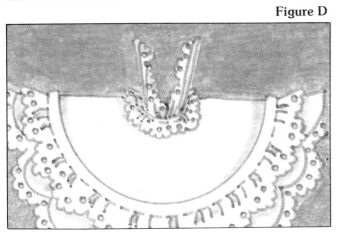

Figure C

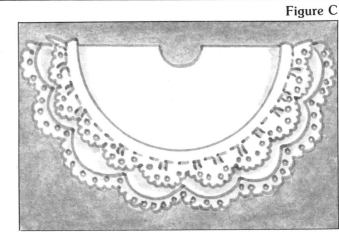

Figure D

Figure E

133

Figure I

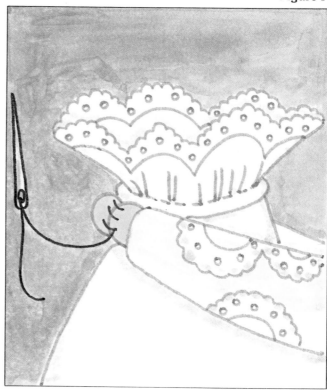

Making the arms and sleeves

1. To make the arms, cut a 1-inch-wide strip of pantyhose, 10 inches long.

2. Form a strand of polyester fiberfill about 11 inches long and ½ inch in diameter.

3. Wrap the hose strip around the fiberfill and whipstitch the edges together **(Figure F)**.

4. Tie a thread tightly around the center of the hose tube. Tie the tube 2 more times, ½ inch on either side of the first tie **(Figure G)**.

5. Cut 2 Sleeve pieces from the 5-inch-wide flat lace. Fold each sleeve right sides together and stitch along the seam line.

6. Turn the sleeves right side out and slip them (wide end first) over the ends of the arms. The sleeve seams should be positioned against the whipstitching in the arms **(Figure H)**.

7. Wrap the assembled sleeves and arms around the neckline of the dress. Whipstitch the ends of the arms and sleeves together at the back neckline **(Figure I)**.

Making the head

1. Cut a 4-inch-diameter circle of pantyhose. Wrap the circle around a 2½-inch-diameter ball of polyester fiberfill. Gather the raw edges of the hose at the bottom of the head and tie them together with thread.

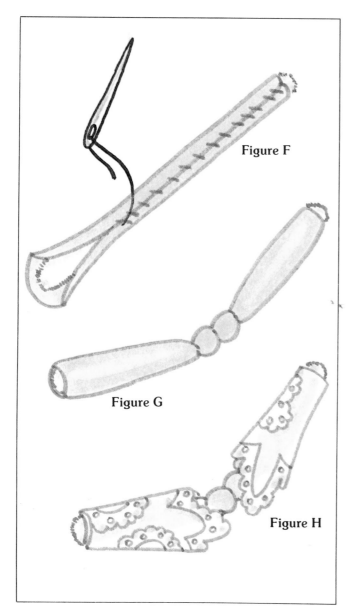

Figure F

Figure G

Figure H

2. Follow the illustrations given in **Figure J** to form the facial features. Use heavy-duty thread and a long sharp needle.

    a. Enter at 1 and exit at 2. Sew a circle of basting stitches approximately ½ inch in diameter, exiting at 3.

    b. Use the tip of the needle to very carefully lift the fiberfill within the circle just enough to make a small bulge. Gently pull the thread until a small round nose appears.

    c. Hold the thread with 1 hand and lock the stitch under the bridge of the nose, exiting at 2.

    d. To form the nostrils, reenter at 2 and exit at 4.

    e. Reenter slightly above 4 and exit at 3.

    f. Reenter at 3 and exit at 5.

    g. Reenter slightly above 5 and exit at 2. Lock the stitch under the bridge of the nose.

    h. To form the eyes, enter at 2 and exit at 6.

    i. Pull the thread over the surface, enter at 2 and exit at 3.

    j. Reenter at 3 and exit at 7.

    k. Pull the thread across the surface, enter at 3 and exit at 2. Gently pull the thread until the eyelid appears, and lock the stitch.

    l. To form the mouth, enter at 2 and exit at 8.

    m. Pull the thread across the surface, enter at 9 and exit at 3. Pull the thread until a smile appears.

    n. Reenter at 3 and exit at 1. Lock the stitch and cut the thread.

3. Draw the lips with a red marker and brush powdered cheek blusher on the cheeks.

4. Draw the eyebrows and eyelashes with a black felt-tip marker.

Making the hair

1. Stitch the free end of the white yarn to the center top of the angel's head using needle and thread.

2. Begin coiling the yarn around the stitched end. Keep the coils flat against the head and glue each coil in place as you work. Continue until the head is covered to the hairline. End the coil at the back neckline. Cut the yarn and stitch the end down.

3. To add the curls to the sides of the face, stitch down the free end of the white yarn with heavy-duty thread. Wrap the yarn around the tip of the needle 5 times and take another stitch (**Figure K**).

4. Repeat step 3 until you have formed a generous cluster of curls on both sides of the head.

Adding the wings

1. Cut the enlarged Wings piece from lace fabric. Pay particular attention to the "place on fold" notation.

2. Soak the lace wings in liquid starch. Allow them to dry flat overnight.

Figure J

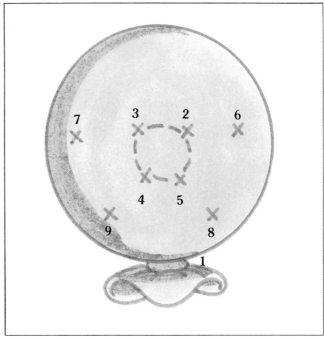

Figure K

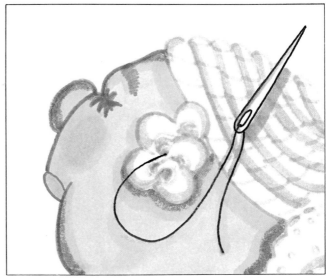

3. Hand stitch 1-inch-wide flat lace along the edges of the wings, folding the lace to lie flat around the curves.

4. Press the completed wings with a hot iron.

5. Whipstitch the center top of the wings to the back neckline of the angel. Stitch down the center of the wings to secure them to the gown.

Christmas Wreath

This bright and cheerful wreath is made from the cardboard collars on egg-shaped pantyhose containers. Covered with fabric remnants and glued together, they make a wonderful wreath for your Christmas door.

Materials

1 yard of red and white polka-dot fabric.
1½ yards of green and white polka-dot ribbon.
9 small white bells with holes through the top (or substitute any small ornaments).
3 yards of narrow red satin ribbon.
Scissors, razor knife, glue, iron, and ironing board.
Heavy-duty clear nylon thread and a long sharp needle.
9 cardboard collars from egg-shaped pantyhose containers.
12-inch length of picture-hanging wire.
Spring-type clothespins and a toothpick.

Covering the collars

1. Use a razor knife to cut the flat bottom out of all 9 cardboard collars.

2. Cut 9 fabric rectangles from the red and white polka-dot fabric, each measuring 5 x 12 inches. These will be the outer covers for the collars.

3. Glue one 5-inch end of the outer cover onto a cardboard collar as shown in **Figure A.** Wrap the cover completely around the outside of the collar and glue the free end down.

4. Wipe glue inside the collar and wrap both long edges of the fabric cover to the inside as shown in **Figure B.** Hold the fabric cover in place with spring-type clothespins until the glue dries completely.

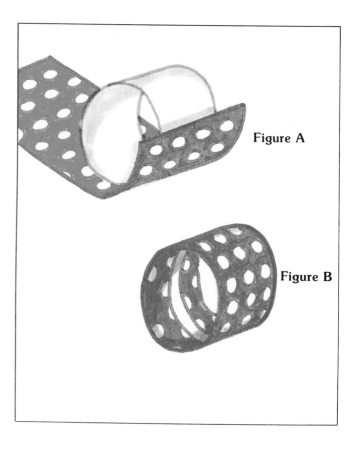

Figure A

Figure B

Figure C

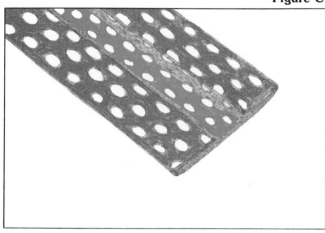

Figure D

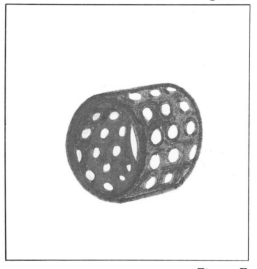

5. Cut 9 fabric rectangles from the red and white polka-dot fabric, each 3 x 10 inches. These will be the inner covers for the cardboard collars.

6. Fold over both long edges of each rectangle ½ inch and press with a steam iron **(Figure C)**.

7. Wipe glue inside the fabric-covered collars, and fit the inner covers around the inside. Use a toothpick to spread glue evenly along the edges **(Figure D)**. Use clothespins to hold the fabric until the glue dries.

Adding the bells

1. Thread a narrow red ribbon through the hole at the top of a bell. Tie the ribbon in a knot to form a hanging loop. The loop should be small enough so that the ornament will hang properly inside the collar **(Figure E)**.

2. Tie a small red satin bow and glue it to the front of the bell.

3. Sew the ribbon loop to the inside of the fabric-covered collar. Use heavy-duty thread and sew completely through the collar. Lock the stitch and cut the thread.

4. Repeat steps 1 through 3 for the remaining 8 bells, sewing 1 inside each of the collars.

Figure E

Finishing

1. Place the completed collars on a flat surface and arrange them in a circle. Be sure to turn the collars so that the bells will hang properly when the wreath is finished.

2. Wipe glue on the outside of the collars where they meet, and clip them together with clothespins until the glue dries.

3. Hand tack the collars together at the front and back edges using a needle and heavy-duty thread.

4. Thread a 12-inch length of picture-hanging wire through the top center collar and twist the ends together at the back of the wreath. Leave a little slack to allow for hanging the finished wreath.

5. Tie a bow with the green and white polka-dot ribbon, following the illustrations given in **Figure F.**

6. Hand tack the completed bow to the top of the wreath.

Figure F

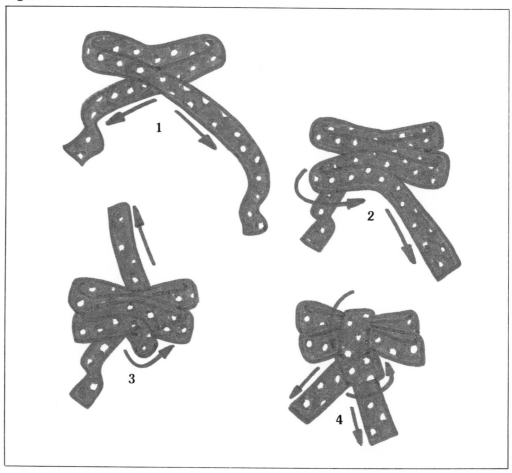

KITCHEN SPICE
... added flavorings where you cook

Kitchen Witch

According to Norwegian folklore, if you place this witch in your kitchen she will prevent pots from boiling over, cakes from falling, and roasts from burning.

Materials

¼ yard of dark calico fabric.
12 x 14-inch piece of blue fabric.
5 x 10-inch piece of striped or checked fabric.
5 x 16-inch piece of brown fabric.
2 small black beads.
¼-inch-diameter dowel rod, 8 inches long.
Small amount of black yarn.
1 leg of dark-colored pantyhose.
Several lengths of ordinary broom straw.
Polyester fiberfill.
Heavy duty nylon thread, needle, straight pins, sewing machine, and scissors.
Pencil and paper to enlarge the patterns.
Glue, iron, and ironing board.

Cutting the pattern pieces

1. Enlarge the pattern pieces given in **Figure A** to full size.

2. Use the full-size patterns to cut the following: 2 Hat pieces from blue fabric; 2 Head pieces from pantyhose; 2 Body pieces and 2 Arm pieces from dark calico fabric; 4 Leg pieces from striped fabric; and 4 Boot pieces from brown fabric.

Making the body

1. Pin the bottom edge of 1 Head piece to the top of 1 Body piece, placing right sides together. Stitch the seam and press it toward the Body **(Figure B).**

2. Cut and place four 3-inch-long strands of black yarn even with the raw edge on each side of the Head. Place the wide edge of 1 Hat piece (right side face down) on the Head, with the raw edges even **(Figure C).** Pin together and stitch.

3. Repeat steps 1 and 2 for the remaining Body, Head, and Hat, adding 8 additional strands of yarn evenly spaced across the back of the head **(Figure D).**

Arms

1. Fold 1 Arm piece lengthwise with right sides together, and sew a ¼-inch seam **(Figure E).**

2. Fold over a ¼-inch-wide hem at one end and press. Stuff the arm lightly, leaving ½ inch unstuffed at the un-hemmed end.

3. To form the hand, cut a 4-inch-diameter circle of hose and place it over a 2½-inch ball of fiberfill. Gather the raw edges of the hose together and tie them with a piece of yarn **(Figure F).**

4. To form the first finger, thread a needle with nylon thread and insert it close to the gathered area at the bottom of the hand. Push the needle diagonally through the hand and exit at the top and to one side **(Figure G).** This exit point will be the base of the first finger.

5. Pinch up a bulge at the top of the "hand." Wrap the thread across the bulge. Enter the needle on the opposite side and exit at the base of the finger where you began. Pull the thread tightly to form 1 finger. Lock the stitch.

Figure A

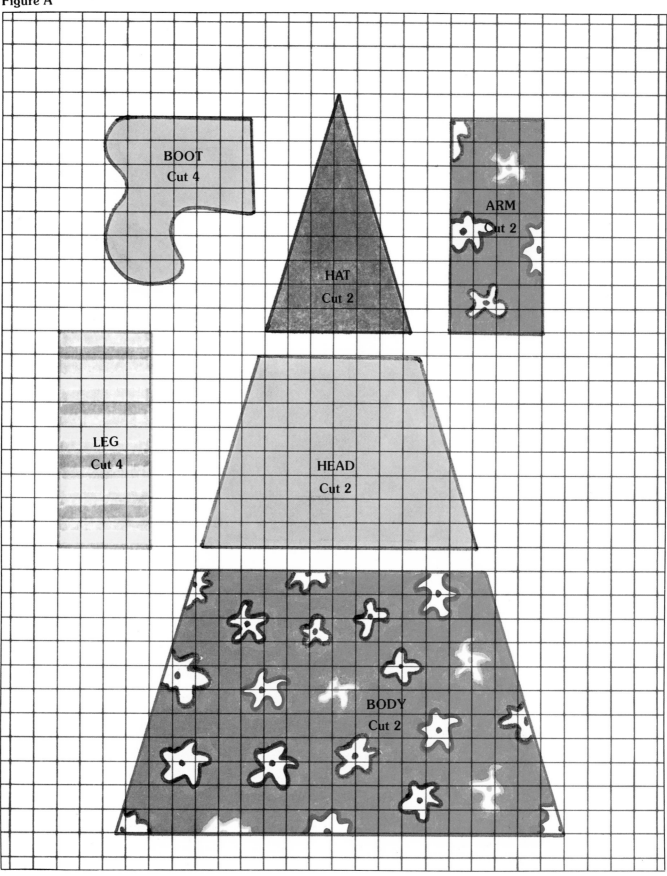

BOOT
Cut 4

HAT
Cut 2

ARM
Cut 2

LEG
Cut 4

HEAD
Cut 2

BODY
Cut 2

Figure B

Figure C

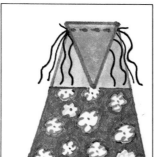

Figure D

Figure E

Figure F

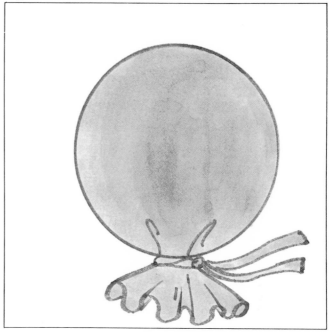

Figure G

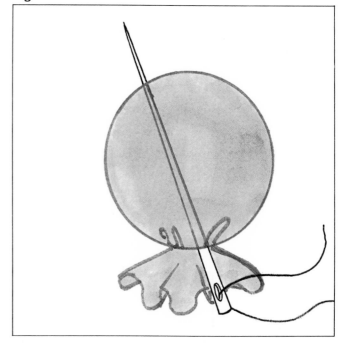

6. Enter at the point where you just exited. Take a ½-inch stitch under the surface and exit at the base of the next finger.

7. Repeat steps 5 and 6 twice to make a total of 3 fingers, each spaced ½ inch apart **(Figure H)**. Exit the needle at the bottom gathers and lock the stitch.

8. Place the gathered end of the hand into the hemmed arm opening **(Figure I)**. Sew gathering stitches around the wrist. Draw the stitches tightly to form a gathered cuff, and lock your stitches.

9. With right sides together, pin the raw edges of the arms to the side seam allowance of the Body **(Figure J)**. Stitch the assembled front and back of the witch together. Match the side seams, and leave the bottom open and unstitched.

10. Turn the witch right side out and stuff, leaving a ½-inch seam allowance unstuffed at the bottom edge.

Sewing the legs

1. Stitch 1 Leg and 1 Boot piece right sides together, and press the seam open **(Figure K)**. Repeat for the remaining 3 Leg and Boot pieces.

2. Place 2 of the seamed legs right sides together and stitch, leaving the leg tops open **(Figure L)**. Repeat for the remaining seamed legs.

3. Clip corners and curves, and turn the finished legs right side out. Stuff the boot portions tightly. Stuff the leg portions until they are round, leaving the top ½ inch unstuffed.

4. Pin the top of the legs to the front side of the body with the boot toes pointing to the body. Stitch ¼ inch from the edge **(Figure M)**.

5. Turn ¼ inch to the inside on the bottom of the body and whipstitch the 2 folded edges together.

Figure H

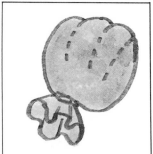

Figure I

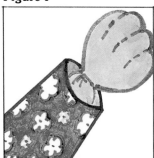

Figure J

Figure K

Figure L

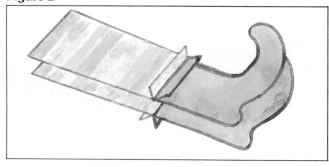

Figure M

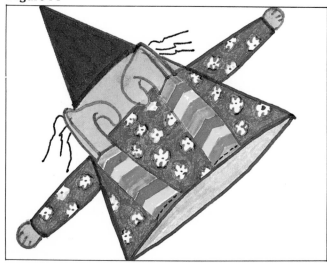

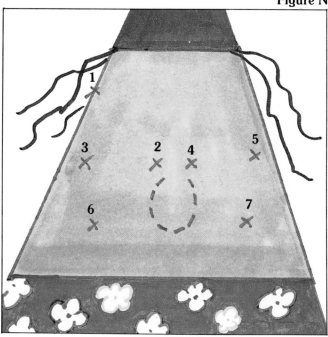

Figure N

Forming the face

1. To form the facial features, use a long needle and nylon thread. Refer to the entry and exit points given in **Figure N** carefully. For more accurate facial features, lightly draw each of the points on the witch's face. The stitches must be exaggerated, since a 2-inch-wide stitch will draw up to ½ inch wide. The tighter you pull the thread, the less the stitches will show.

    a. Enter needle at point 1 and exit at point 2.

    b. Reenter needle at 2 and exit at 3.

    c. Enter at 2 and exit at 4.

    d. Reenter at 4 and exit at 5.

    e. Enter at 4 and exit at 2. Pull the thread tightly and take another stitch to lock the thread.

2. Pinch up the nose to form a ridge. Wrap thread around the pinched nose and enter at 4. Exit at 2 and pull the thread to draw up the nose. Lock the stitch.

3. Raise the cheeks by gently lifting the fiberfill beneath the hose with the tip of your needle.

4. Reenter at 2 and exit at 6. Enter at 7 and exit at 2. Pull the thread to form a toothless grin. Hold the pulled thread with 1 hand and lock the stitch.

5. Glue the black beads in the eye indentations.

Finishing

1. To "twizzle" the hair, untwist the yarn and separate each strand.

2. To make the broom, gather pieces of broomstraw around a wooden dowel rod. Wrap the entire piece with an 8-inch piece of yarn and tie a knot. Glue the finished broom to the left hand.

Katie T. Cozy & Tea Container

Plump little Katie will serve your tea piping hot and see that it doesn't cool down all during tea time. Her matching container will hold tea bags in style.

Materials

1½ pairs of wine-colored heavy "winter" pantyhose.
½ pair of regular pantyhose in a light color.
½ pound of polyester fiberfill.
⅔ yard of 1-inch-wide white eyelet trim.
3-inch square of white cotton fabric.
½ yard of ½-inch-wide white ribbon.
Small amount of brown fiber.
Beige heavy-duty drapery thread and a long sharp needle.
Wine and black sewing thread.
Empty plastic butter or margarine bowl (2 pound size).
Black and red felt-tip markers, powdered cheek blusher, 2 black beads.
Scissors, glue, steam iron, and ironing board.

Making the cozy

1. Cut 1 pair of wine-colored pantyhose in half, separating it into 2 legs. Cut off the toe on each leg and cut each leg open along the inseam to form 2 long flat pieces **(Figure A)**.

2. Press 1 flat piece gently using a steam iron on low heat, and cut in half horizontally **(Figure B)**.

3. Stitch the 2 horizontal halves together down the side seams to form a tube, stretching the hose gently as you sew to retain the elasticity.

4. Fold the tube in half inside itself so that the raw edges are together. The stitched seams are now on the inside of a double layer **(Figure C)**.

5. Gently stuff polyester fiberfill inside the folded layers, working through the opening between the raw edges.

Figure A

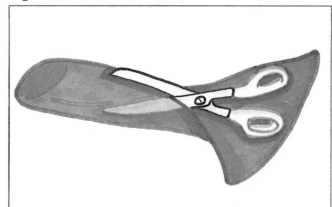

Figure B

Figure C

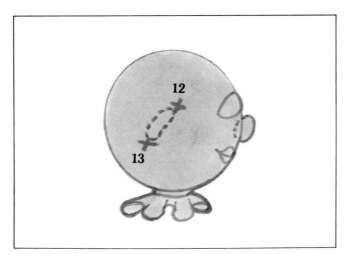

Figure F

Figure D

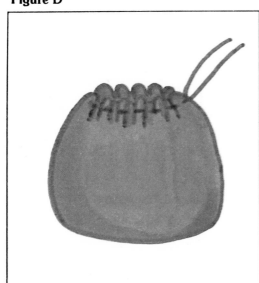

6. Gather the raw edges on both layers together using heavy-duty thread. Pull the gathering threads to draw the raw edges together **(Figure D).** Gently tuck the remaining gathers inside so they are no longer visible.

Making the head

1. Cut a 6-inch-diameter circle from regular pantyhose. Wrap the circle around a 4-inch-diameter ball of polyester fiberfill. Gather the raw edges of the hose at the bottom of the head and tie them together with thread.

2. Follow the illustrations given in **Figure E** to form the facial features. Use heavy-duty thread and a long sharp needle.

    a. Enter at 1 and exit at 2. Sew a circle of basting stitches approximately ½ inch in diameter, exiting at 3.

    b. Use the tip of the needle to very carefully lift the fiberfill within the circle just enough to make a small bulge. Gently pull the thread until a small round nose appears.

    c. Hold the thread with 1 hand and lock the stitch under the bridge of the nose, exiting at 2.

    d. To form the nostrils, reenter at 2 and exit at 4.

    e. Reenter slightly above 4 and exit at 3.

    f. Reenter at 3 and exit at 5.

    g. Reenter slightly above 5 and exit at 2. Lock the stitch under the bridge of the nose.

    h. To form the eyes, enter at 2 and exit at 6.

    i. Pull the thread over the surface, enter at 2 and exit at 3.

    j. Reenter at 3 and exit at 7.

    k. Pull the thread across the surface, enter at 3 and exit at 2. Gently pull the thread until the bottom line of the eyes appears and lock the stitch.

    l. To form the mouth, enter at 2 and exit at 8.

    m. Pull the thread across the surface, enter at 9 and exit at 3. Pull the thread until a smile appears.

    n. Reenter at 3 and exit at 1. Lock the stitch and cut the thread.

Figure E

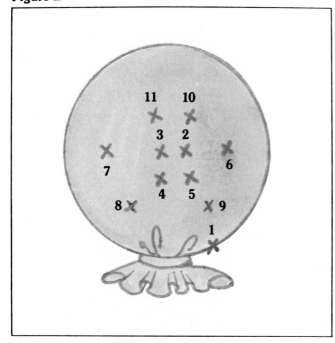

3. Draw the lips with a red marker and brush powdered cheek blusher on the cheeks.

4. To complete the eyes, thread a long sharp needle with black thread. Again, follow the illustrations given in **Figure E.** Enter at 1 and exit at 6. Pull the thread across the surface, enter at 10 and exit at 1. Repeat the process on the other side, exiting at 7 and entering at 11.

5. Glue black beads on the inside corners of the eye identations.

6. Draw eyebrows over the eyes using a black marker.

7. Thread the needle again with beige heavy-duty thread and follow the entry and exit points illustrated in **Figure F** to form the ears.

   a. Pinch up a small ridge at an angle on the side of the head just below the eyeline. Enter at 1 and exit at 12. Stitch back and forth under the ridge until an ear forms.

   b. Exit at 13 and lock the stitch.

   c. Reenter at 13 and exit at 1. Lock the stitch and cut the thread.

8. Repeat step 7 on the opposite side of the head, reversing the angle to form the other ear.

9. Glue brown fiber on top of the head, twisting it into a bun at the back.

10. Cut and glue a 4-inch length of white eyelet just in front of the hair bun, curving it slightly to look like a maid's cap.

11. Glue the completed head to the top of the cozy, placing it over the gathers on the top.

12. Glue the remaining 20-inch length of eyelet trim to the cozy, dipping it lower in the front than in the back **(Figure G).**

Adding the hands

1. Form a 2-inch-diameter ball of fiberfill and cover it with a 3-inch-diameter circle cut from regular pantyhose. Gather the raw edges at the bottom and tie them together with thread.

2. Glue or stitch the ball to the front of the cozy, placing at the center front just under the eyelet trim.

3. Thread a needle with heavy-duty thread and follow the illustrations given in **Figure H** to form the fingers.

   a. Enter the needle at 1 and exit at 2.

   b. Take a vertical stitch across the center on the surface of the ball to divide it into 2 equal parts. Enter at 3, pull the thread tightly, and lock the stitch.

   c. Take 4 evenly-spaced small stitches on each side of the dividing line and pull the thread to form little fingers as shown in the illustration. Exit at 3 and lock the stitch.

4. Hem all 4 edges of the white cotton square. Use a black laundry marker to write "Tea Time" in the center of the hemmed square. Whipstitch the square to the center front of the cozy, just above the eyelet trim.

Figure G

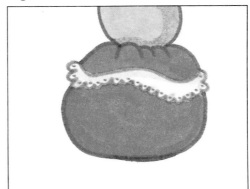

Figure H

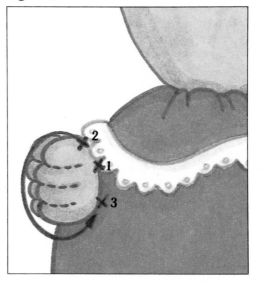

Making the tea bag container

1. The tea container is made in exactly the same manner as the cozy (steps 2 through 6 under "Making the cozy") using the remaining flat pantyhose leg. The difference is that the gathers are placed on the bottom of the container after finishing.

2. To make the lid for the tea container, repeat the same procedure as the tea cozy, through step 5. Use only half as much fiberfill stuffing.

3. Gather the 2 layers together 4 inches from the raw edges. Pull the gathering thread and lock the stitch. Tuck the raw edges on the gathers to the inside. Tie a bow around the gathers, leaving a top knot.

4. Flatten the lid with your hands to fit the top of the container.

5. Set the plastic bowl inside the container and gently stretch the hose up and around the bowl.

Fantasy Flowers

These fabulous flowers are made with white hose and spray-painted to coordinate with any decor. And since they require no light, you can place them in a corner where live plants won't grow.

Materials

1 pair of nurse's white pantyhose.
Four 12-inch-long pipe cleaners for each flower, 3 white and 1 green.
One 12-inch-long green pipe cleaner for each fern frond.
Spray paint in the following colors: yellow, blue, orange, and green.
Dried baby's breath and a basket container.
Two 12-inch square pieces of felt, 1 white and 1 green.
Spring-type clothespins.
1 yard of 1-inch-wide decorative ribbon.
Scissors, glue, and newspapers.

Making the flowers

1. Cut 6 petal pieces from white pantyhose, each 2 inches square.

2. Bend a white pipe cleaner into a double petal shape as shown in **Figure A**.

3. Wipe glue around the edges of the double petal. Stretch a hose petal piece flat against the glue. Hold the hose in place with a clothespin until the glue dries **(Figure B)**.

4. Remove the clothespin and trim away the excess hose around the outer edges.

5. Place the completed double petal flat on a piece of newspaper and spray paint one side in the color of your choice. Allow the paint to dry.

6. Turn the double petal over and paint the other side. Again, allow the paint to dry.

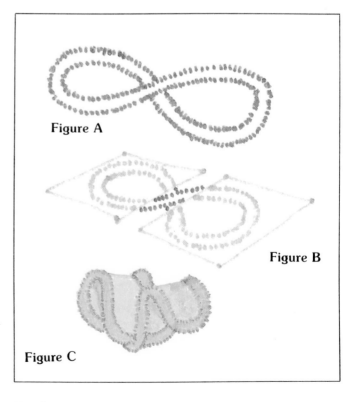

Figure A

Figure B

Figure C

7. Carefully fold the double petal together in the center, then bend each petal down as shown in **Figure C**.

148

8. Stack 3 double petals on top of one another to form the flower.

9. Fold a green pipe cleaner in half and place the fold over the 3 double petals as shown in **Figure D.** Twist the 2 ends of the pipe cleaner together tightly beneath the petals to form the stem.

Adding the calyx and flower center

1. A full-size pattern for the calyx is given in **Figure E.** Trace the pattern and cut 1 from green felt.

2. Insert the pipe cleaner stem through the hole in the center of the felt calyx. Pull the calyx up under the petals and glue it in place.

3. To form the flower center, cut a 1-inch square of white felt. Cut ½-inch-deep fringe across 1 side of the square **(Figure F).** Roll up the felt square along the uncut edge. Glue the rolled edge to the inside of the flower.

Making the fern fronds

1. To make 1 frond, cut a strip of white hose 7 x 4 inches. Wipe glue on all but the bottom 2 inches of a green pipe cleaner.

2. Stretch a strip of hose and center it over the glued portion of the pipe cleaner. Hold the hose in place with clothespins until the glue dries. The stretching action of the hose will curve the pipe cleaner into a frond shape **(Figure G).**

3. Spray both sides of the completed frond with green paint. Allow the paint to dry.

4. Clip the completed frond with scissors every ½ inch along each side to form fringe.

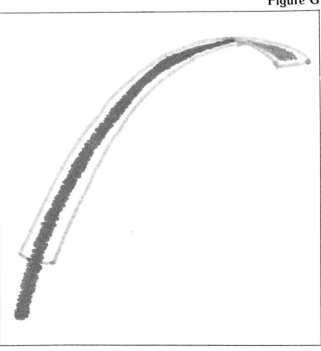

Finishing

1. Make as many flowers and fronds as you wish for your arrangement. You can make smaller flowers for your arrangement by using 2 double petals rather than 3.

2. Arrange the finished flowers and fronds in a basket container. Add baby's breath to fill out the arrangement.

3. Tie a ribbon bow on the side of the basket.

Taste Makes Waist

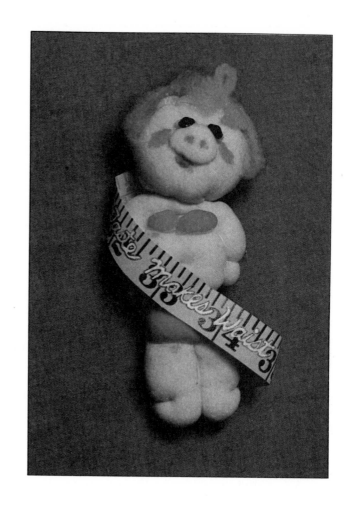

If you attach this well-rounded character to your refrigerator door, you won't be tempted to "pig out" on goodies.

Figure A

Materials

1 leg cut from nude-colored pantyhose.
Small amount of polyester fiberfill.
Heavy-duty white thread and a long sharp needle.
Red felt-tip marker.
2 small black beads.
6-inch length of thin red yarn.
Small amount of yellow fiber.
2 small magnets.
10-inch section cut from a measuring tape.
3 x 6-inch rectangle of white felt.
White acrylic paint and a small paint brush.
Scissors, pencil, and glue.

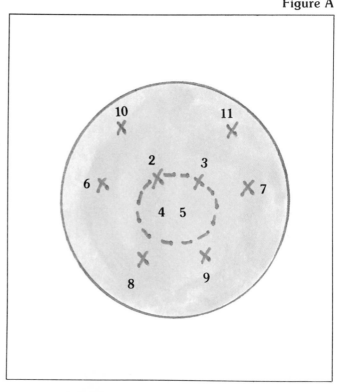

Forming the head and body

1. Cut a 3-inch-diameter circle of pantyhose. Wrap the circle around a 1-inch-diameter ball of polyester fiberfill. Gather the raw edges of the hose at the bottom and tie them together with thread. Flatten the ball as much as possible to form the head.

2. Make 2 additional hose-covered balls and flatten them as you did for the head in step 1. These will be the body and legs.

150

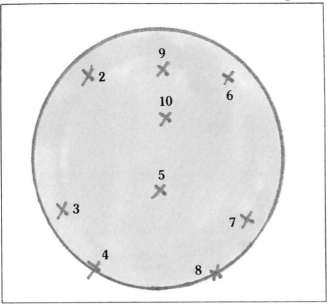

Sewing the facial features

1. Follow the entry and exit points illustrated in **Figure A** to form the facial features on the head. Place the gathered portion of the hose at the back of the head.

    a. Enter at the back in the gathered area and exit at 2.

    b. Enter at 3 and sew a circle of basting stitches in the center of the face about ½-inch in diameter, ending at 2.

    c. Pull the thread to form the nose and lock the stitch. To form the nostrils, reenter at 2 and exit at 4.

    d. Reenter at 4 and exit at 5.

    e. Reenter at 5 and exit at 2.

    f. To make the eyes, reenter at 2 and exit at 6.

    g. Enter at 2 and exit at 3.

    h. Reenter at 3 and exit at 7.

    i. Enter at 3 and exit at 2. Pull the thread tightly to form the eyes. Lock the stitch under the bridge of the nose.

    j. To form the mouth, enter at 2 and exit at 8.

    k. Enter at 9 and exit at 2. Pull the thread and lock the stitch.

2. Gently raise the fiberfill underneath the nose to form the cheeks, using the tip of the needle.

3. To form the ears, again follow the entry and exit points in Figure A.

    a. Enter at 2 and exit at 10.

    b. Pull the thread up and to the back of the head. Enter behind 10 and exit at 10.

    c. Pull the thread to the left and to the back of the head. Enter behind 10 and exit at 10. Pull the thread to form the ear.

    d. Reenter at 10 and exit at 11.

4. Repeat step 3 at point 11 to form the other ear. Lock the stitch.

5. Glue black beads in the eye indentations.

Sewing the body

1. Follow the entry and exit points illustrated in **Figure B** to form the body using the second hose-covered ball.

    a. Enter at the gathered area on the back and exit at 2.

    b. Enter at 3. Wrap the stitch around the left side. Enter behind 3, and exit at 3.

    c. Enter at 4 and exit at the same point. Wrap the thread to the back and enter behind 3. Exit at 3.

    d. Reenter at 3 and exit at 5.

    e. Reenter at 5 and exit at 6.

    f. Enter at 7 and wrap the thread around the right side to the back. Enter behind 7 and exit at 7.

    g. Enter at 8 and exit at the same point. Wrap the thread to the back and enter behind 7. Exit at 7.

    h. Reenter at 7 and exit at 9.

    i. Enter at 2 and exit at 10.

    j. Enter at 6 and exit at 9.

    k. Enter at 10 and exit at 2.

    l. Enter at 10 and exit at 9.

    m. Enter at 6 and exit behind the body.

2. Pull the thread and lock the stitch.

Figure E

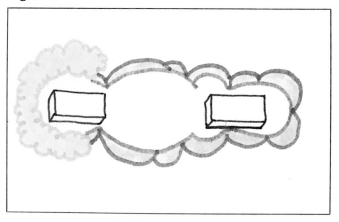

Figure C

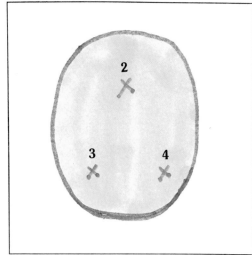

Figure D

Sewing the legs

1. Follow the entry and exit points illustrated in **Figure C** to form the legs. Use the remaining hose-covered ball.

   a. Enter at the gathered area in the back and exit at 2. Wrap the thread around the right side to the back. Reenter behind 2 and exit at 2.

   b. Wrap the thread around the left side to the back. Enter behind 2 and exit at 2.

   c. Wrap the thread around the bottom to the back. Enter behind 2 and exit at 2.

   d. Reenter at 2 and exit on the back. Pull the thread and lock the stitch.

   e. Enter on the back and exit at 3.

   f. Wrap the thread around the left side to the back. Enter behind 3 and exit at 3.

   g. Reenter at 3 and exit at 4.

   h. Wrap the thread around the right side. Enter behind 4 and exit at 4.

   i. Reenter at 4 and exit on the back. Lock the stitch.

2. Whipstitch the 3 parts together, placing the head on the top, the body in the middle, and the legs on the bottom **(Figure D).**

Finishing

1. Arrange the fiber hair around the face and glue it in place. Tie a small red yarn bow and tack it to the hair.

2. Color the cheeks, lips, and bikini with the red felt-tip marker. Add a touch of red marker to the cheeks.

3. Wrap a section of measuring tape around the body, beginning and ending it on the back. Glue the tape in place.

4. Paint "Taste Makes Waist" across the front of the measuring tape using white acrylic paint and a small paint brush. Instructions for fabric painting are given in the "Tips and Techniques" section at the front of this book.

5. Trace the outline of the finished figure onto white felt. Cut the white felt inside the traced outline. Glue the felt cutout to the back of the figure to cover the gathered hose **(Figure E).**

6. Glue 2 magnets to the back of the figure, placing 1 at the bottom and 1 at the top.

Hot Pad, Drink Coaster, & Napkin Ring

Here are 3 clever additions to your kitchen that you can whip up in just a few minutes each. They're also great for small "thank you" gifts to friends.

Materials

For the hot pad:
    1 pair of brown heavy "winter" pantyhose.
    Scrap piece of regular pantyhose.
    Small amount of polyester fiberfill.
    A brown felt-tip marker.

For the drink coaster:
    1 brown opaque knee-high hose.
    Scrap piece of nurse's white hose.
    3-inch square of heavy brown fabric.
    Small amount of polyester fiberfill.
    A yellow felt-tip marker.

For the napkin ring:
    1 brown opaque knee-high hose.
    Scrap piece of nurse's white hose.
    Small amount of polyester fiberfill.
    A yellow felt-tip marker.
Scissors, heavy-duty thread, and a long sharp needle.

Figure A

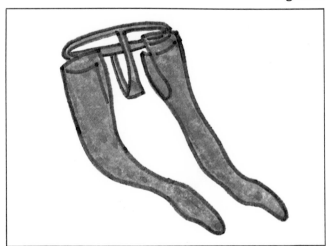

Making the hot pad

1. Cut the 2 leg portions from a pair of brown heavy "winter" pantyhose, eliminating all seams as shown in **Figure A.**

153

Figure C

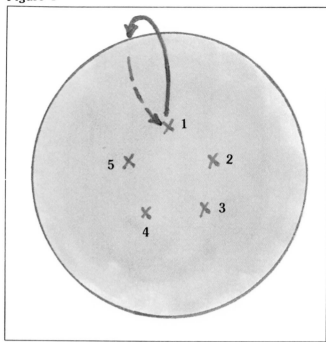

Making the flower

1. To make the flower, form a small ball of polyester fiberfill and wrap it with a 2-inch-diameter circle cut from regular pantyhose. Gather the raw edges of the hose together and tie them with thread.

2. Flatten the ball so the gathers are on the underside. Follow the illustrations given in **Figure C** to form the flower. Use a long sharp needle and heavy-duty thread.

    a. Enter on the back at the gathered area and exit at 1.

    b. Wrap the thread around the edge to the back. Enter behind 1 and exit at 1 again.

    c. Enter at 2 and exit on the back.

    d. Wrap the thread around the edge to the front. Enter at 2 and exit on the back.

    e. Reenter on the back and exit at 2.

    f. Enter at 3 and exit on the back.

    g. Wrap the thread around the edge to the front. Enter at 3 and exit on the back.

    h. Reenter on the back and exit at 3.

    i. Enter at 4 and exit on the back.

    j. Wrap the thread around the edge to the front. Enter at 4 and exit on the back.

    k. Enter on the back and exit at 4.

    l. Enter at 5 and exit on the back.

    m. Wrap the thread around the edge to the front. Enter at 5 and exit on the back.

    n. Reenter on the back and exit at 5.

    o. Enter at 1 and exit on the back. Lock the stitch and cut the thread.

3. Color the center of the flower using a brown marker.

4. Hand tack the flower to the end of the coil.

Figure B

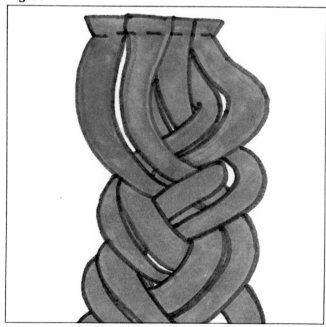

2. Cut each of the 2 legs into 3 long pieces (a total of 6 pieces from 2 legs).

3. Place the ends of all 6 strips together and sew them securely.

4. Divide the strips into 3 groups of 2 strips each and braid them tightly together **(Figure B)**.

5. Coil the braid on a flat surface, stitching the coils together as you work. The stitched side will be the underside of the finished hot pad.

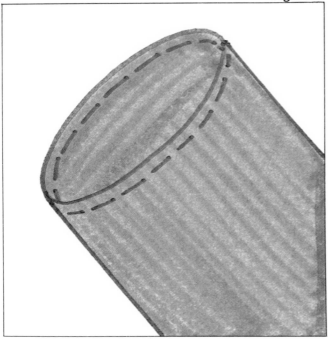

Figure D

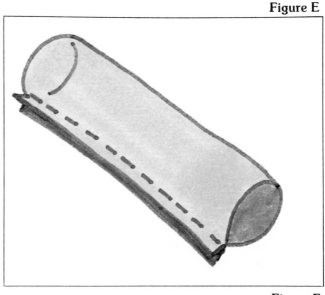

Figure E

Making the drink coaster

1. Cut the top from a brown opaque knee-high hose, ¼ inch below the ribbing.

2. Cut a 3-inch-diameter circle of heavy brown fabric.

3. Turn the hose top wrong side out. Sew the fabric circle to the cut edge of the hose top **(Figure D)**. Turn the coaster right side out.

4. Make a flower using a scrap piece of white hose. Follow steps 1 and 2 under "Making the flower".

5. Color the center of the flower using a yellow marker.

6. Hand tack the flower to the top of the drink coaster.

Making the napkin ring

1. Cut the top 2 inches from a brown opaque knee-high hose. Cut the hose along 1 side and open it out flat. Cut off a 5-inch length to use for the napkin ring.

2. Fold the 5-inch hose lengthwise and sew a ¼-inch-wide seam down the long side to form a tube **(Figure E)**. Turn the tube right side out.

3. Turn the raw edges of the tube to the inside, and whipstitch the ends together using heavy-duty thread **(Figure F)**.

4. Make a flower using a scrap piece of white hose. Follow steps 1 and 2 under "Making the flower."

5. Color the center of the flower using a yellow marker.

6. Hand tack the flower to the napkin ring on top of the stitched seam.

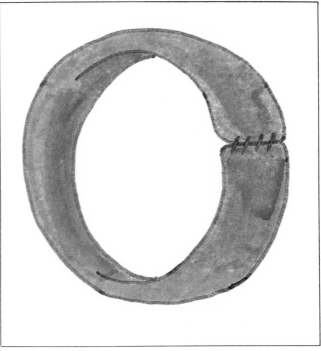

Figure F

Casserole Carrier

This snappy looking casserole dish cover will carry your contribution to the potluck supper in style.

Making the bottom

1. To make the bottom of the casserole cover, cut the ribbed top and the toe seam from 2 knee-high hose.

2. Cut along 1 side of each hose and open them flat.

3. Sew the 2 flat hose pieces together on all 4 sides to form the bottom, leaving a 2-inch opening unstitched on 1 side **(Figure A)**. Stretch the hose gently as you stitch to maintain the elasticity.

4. Turn the stitched hose so the seam is on the inside.

5. Lightly stuff the bottom with polyester fiberfill, and whipstitch the opening closed.

Making the sides and ends

1. To make 1 side for the casserole cover, cut the ribbed top and the top seam from 1 knee-high hose.

2. Cut along both sides of the hose to divide it in half. Fold each half lengthwise and stitch a ¼-inch seam down the long side and across 1 end to form a tube **(Figure B)**. Remember to stretch the hose gently as you sew.

Materials

8½ x 11-inch glass casserole dish.
3 pairs of dark blue opaque knee-high hose.
3 yards of red-and-white plaid ribbon.
1 yard of narrow white grosgrain ribbon.
2 large white buttons.
White embroidery thread and a needle large enough to accommodate 1 full strand of embroidery thread.
½ pound of polyester fiberfill and scissors.
Heavy-duty blue thread and a long sharp needle.

Note: The finished casserole carrier will appear to be too small; however, it will stretch perfectly to fit snugly around an 8½ x 11-inch casserole dish.

Figure A

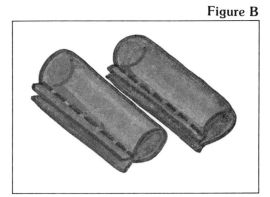
Figure B

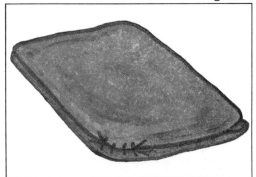
Figure C

3. Turn the stitched tubes so the seams are on the insides.

4. Stuff each tube lightly. Turn the raw edges on the openings to the inside and whipstitch them.

5. Repeat steps 1 through 4 to make the 2 ends for the casserole carrier. In step 4, turn the raw edges farther inside than you did for the sides. Use the ends of the carrier bottom as a reference to determine the length for the end tubes.

6. Whipstitch the sides and ends to the carrier bottom.

Making the lid

1. To make the lid, follow the instructions under "Making the bottom" (steps 1 through 5).

2. Tuck the hose to the inside on all 4 corners of the lid and whipstitch the edges together **(Figure C).**

Finishing

1. Stretch the carrier over an 8½ x 11-inch glass casserole dish. Stretch and shape the lid to fit over the top.

2. Whipstitch red-and-white plaid ribbon over all 4 corner seams on the carrier. Turn the raw ends of the ribbon under, and wrap the top of the ribbon inside the carrier.

3. Lace over the ribbon at all 4 corners by sewing large stitches with embroidery thread **(Figure D).**

4. Whipstitch narrow white grosgrain ribbon around the edges of the lid. Lace the ribbon with large embroidery stitches as you did for the corners.

5. Whipstitch red-and-white plaid ribbon lengthwise across the top of the lid, leaving an extra 4 inches of ribbon at each end to form the loops.

6. Fold the ribbon ends into loops and hand tack them in place **(Figure E).**

7. Sew buttons on the ends of the carrier to fit the ribbon loops.

8. Tie a red-and-white plaid ribbon bow and sew it to the center of the carrier lid.

Figure D

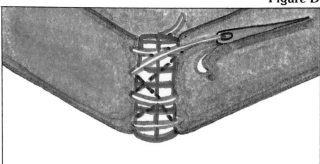

Figure E

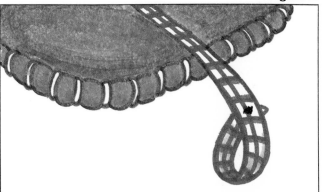

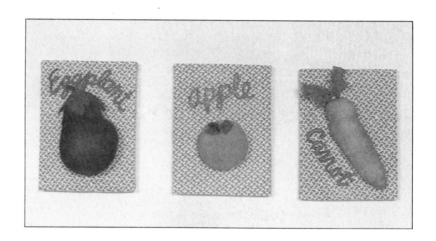

Add a touch of brightness to your kitchen with these cozy pictures. They also make great gifts for a housewarming.

Kitchen Pictures

Materials

Three 1-inch-thick wood boards, each 6 x 8 inches.
3 pieces of lightweight white cardboard, each 5¾ x 7¾ inches.
½ yard of brown-and-white calico fabric.
Small piece of dark green felt.
1 leg of nurse's white pantyhose.
1 wine-colored opaque knee-high hose.
Spray paint in the following colors: wine, orange, green, and red.
Small paint brush and a black laundry marker.
Tracing paper, pencil, and carbon paper.
2 pipe cleaners; 1 brown and 1 green.
¼ pound of polyester fiberfill.
3 sawtooth picture hangers.
Glue, scissors, white glue, and spring-type clothespins.
Heavy-duty thread and a long sharp needle.
A stack of books (or other heavy weight), and newspapers.

Covering the boards

1. Cut a 10 x 12-inch rectangle of calico fabric.

2. Wipe a thin layer of white glue on the front and sides of 1 board.

3. Carefully center the fabric rectangle over the front of the board, and smooth it out.

4. Turn the board over and pull the fabric up the sides. Glue the *edges* of the fabric to the back of the board. Cut off the excess fabric and miter the corners as shown in **Figure A.**

Figure A

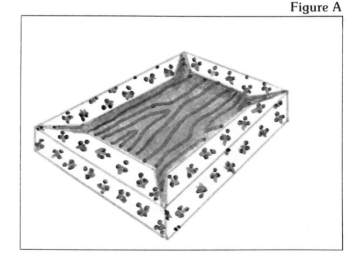

5. Place a stack of books or other heavy weight over the back of the board to hold the fabric edges in place until the glue dries.

6. Glue a 5¾ x 7¾-inch piece of cardboard over the back to hide the fabric edges.

7. Nail a sawtooth picture hanger through the center top of the cardboard.

8. Repeat steps 1 through 7 to complete the remaining 2 boards.

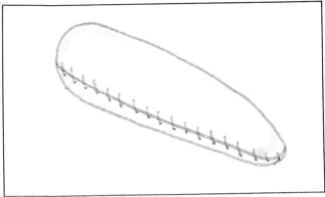

Figure C

Making the carrot

1. Form a cylinder of polyester fiberfill measuring approximately 7 inches long and 3 inches in diameter.

2. Cut a 2 x 6-inch rectangle of white hose. Wrap the hose rectangle around the fiberfill to form a carrot shape as shown in **Figure B**. Whipstitch the raw edges of the hose together on the back of the carrot.

3. Thread the needle with heavy-duty thread and insert it on the back of the carrot at the bottom. Wrap the thread around the carrot several times, ending at the top. Insert the needle at the top back of the carrot. Pull the thread and lock the stitch.

4. Place the finished carrot on newspapers and spray it with orange spray paint. Let the paint dry.

5. To make the carrot top, cut 2 rectangles from white hose, each measuring 2 x 3 inches.

6. Bend a green pipe cleaner in the center to form a V shape. Wipe glue on both ends of the V and stretch the hose rectangles over the glue **(Figure C)**. Hold the hose in place with a clothspin until the glue dries.

7. Remove the clothespins and spray paint the completed leaves green. Allow the paint to dry.

8. Clip the completed leaves with scissors along each side to form fringe **(Figure D)**.

9. Arrange the completed carrot and leaves in the center of a calico-covered board. Glue them in place.

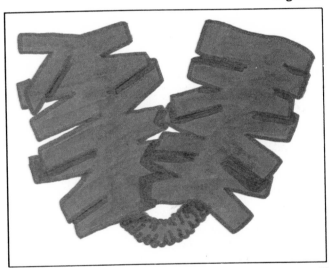

Making the apple

1. Form a ball of polyester fiberfill about 4 inches in diameter.

2. Cut a 6-inch-diameter circle of white hose and wrap it around the fiberfill. Tie the raw edges of the hose together with thread. Flatten the ball to form an apple shape, placing the tied raw edges at the center back.

3. Thread a needle with heavy-duty thread. Enter at the top back of the apple and exit on the front 1 inch from the top as shown in **Figure E**. Reenter on the front and exit on the back. Pull the thread to form an indentation for the stem. Lock the stitch and cut the thread.

4. Place the apple on newspapers and spray it with red paint. Allow the paint to dry.

5. A full-size pattern for the Leaf is given in **Figure F**. Trace the pattern using tracing paper and a pencil. Cut 1 Leaf from green felt.

6. Glue the leaves to the indentation at the top of the apple.

7. Cut a ½-inch length of brown pipe cleaner and glue it to the indentation as a stem.

8. Place the completed apple in the center of a calico-covered board and glue it in place.

159

Figure F

Figure G

APPLE LEAF

Place on Fold

EGGPLANT LEAF

Place on Fold

Making the eggplant

1. Form a ball of polyester fiberfill about 4 inches in diameter.

2. Cut a 6-inch-diameter circle of wine-colored opaque knee-high hose and wrap it around the fiberfill to form a pear-shape as shown in **Figure G.** Whipstitch the raw edges of the hose together on the back.

3. A full-size pattern for the Leaves is given in Figure F. Trace the pattern using tracing paper and a pencil. Cut the Leaves from green felt.

4. Place the eggplant in the center of a calico-covered board with the narrow end up. Glue it in place.

5. Glue the leaves to the top of the eggplant.

Painting

1. Full-size patterns for the lettering are given in Figure F. Trace the patterns and transfer them to the appropriate boards with carbon paper.

2. If you spray a small amount of paint inside the can lid, it will be liquid enough to use with a brush. Paint the lettering on each of the boards with the appropriate color of paint. Let the paint dry.

3. Outline each of the painted letters on both sides with a black laundry marker.